international orange

DANIEL SCHUMANN **international orange**

KERBER

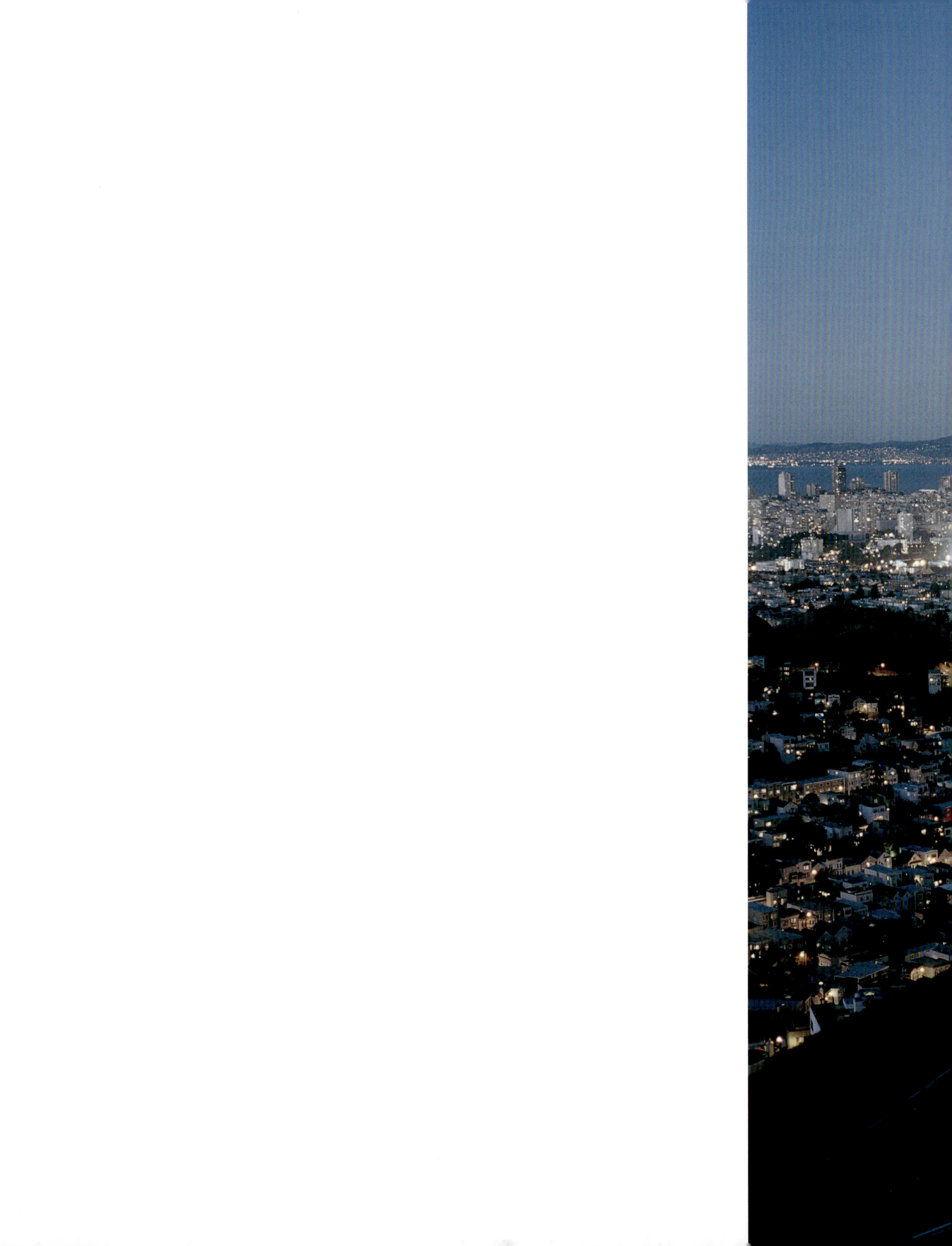

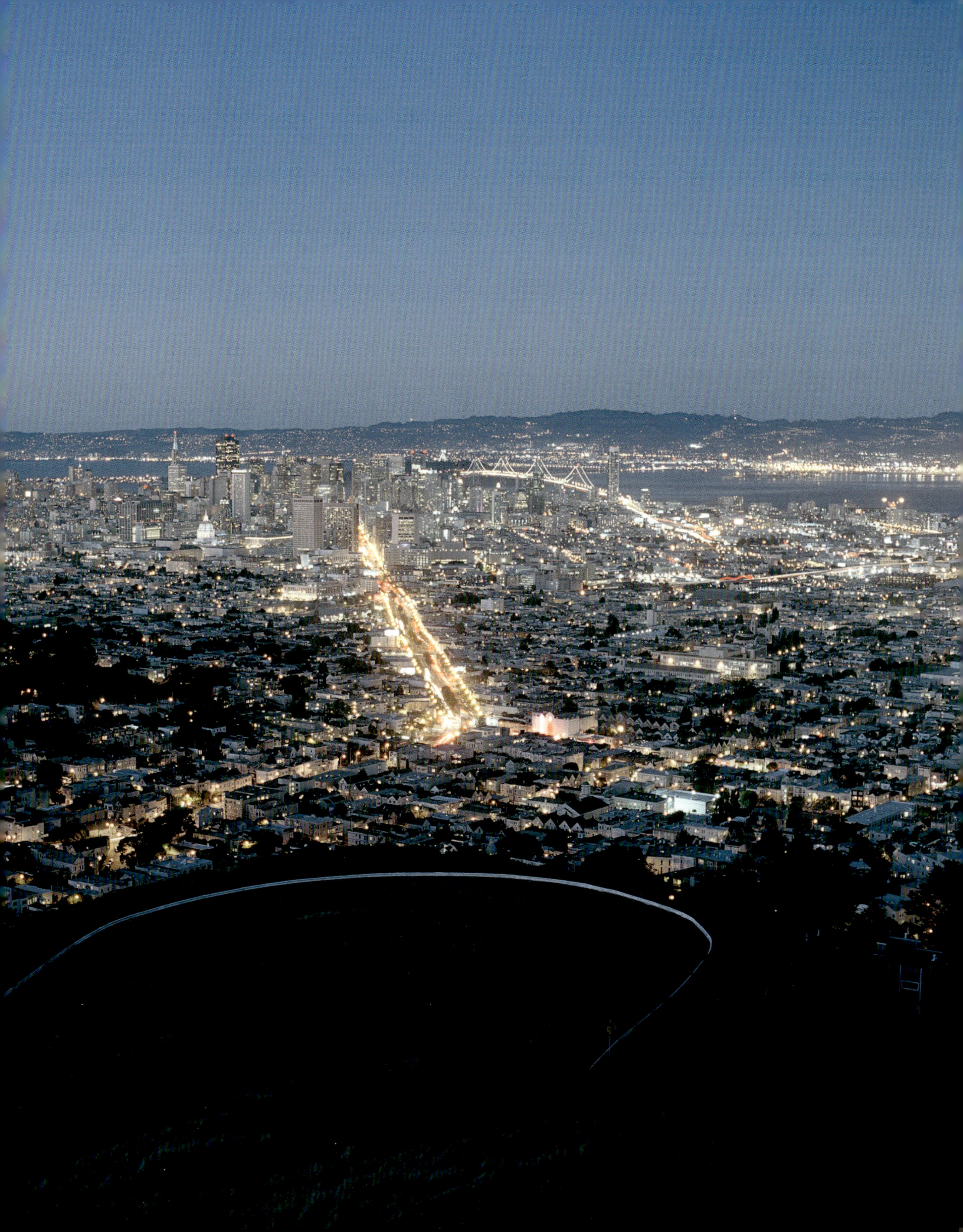

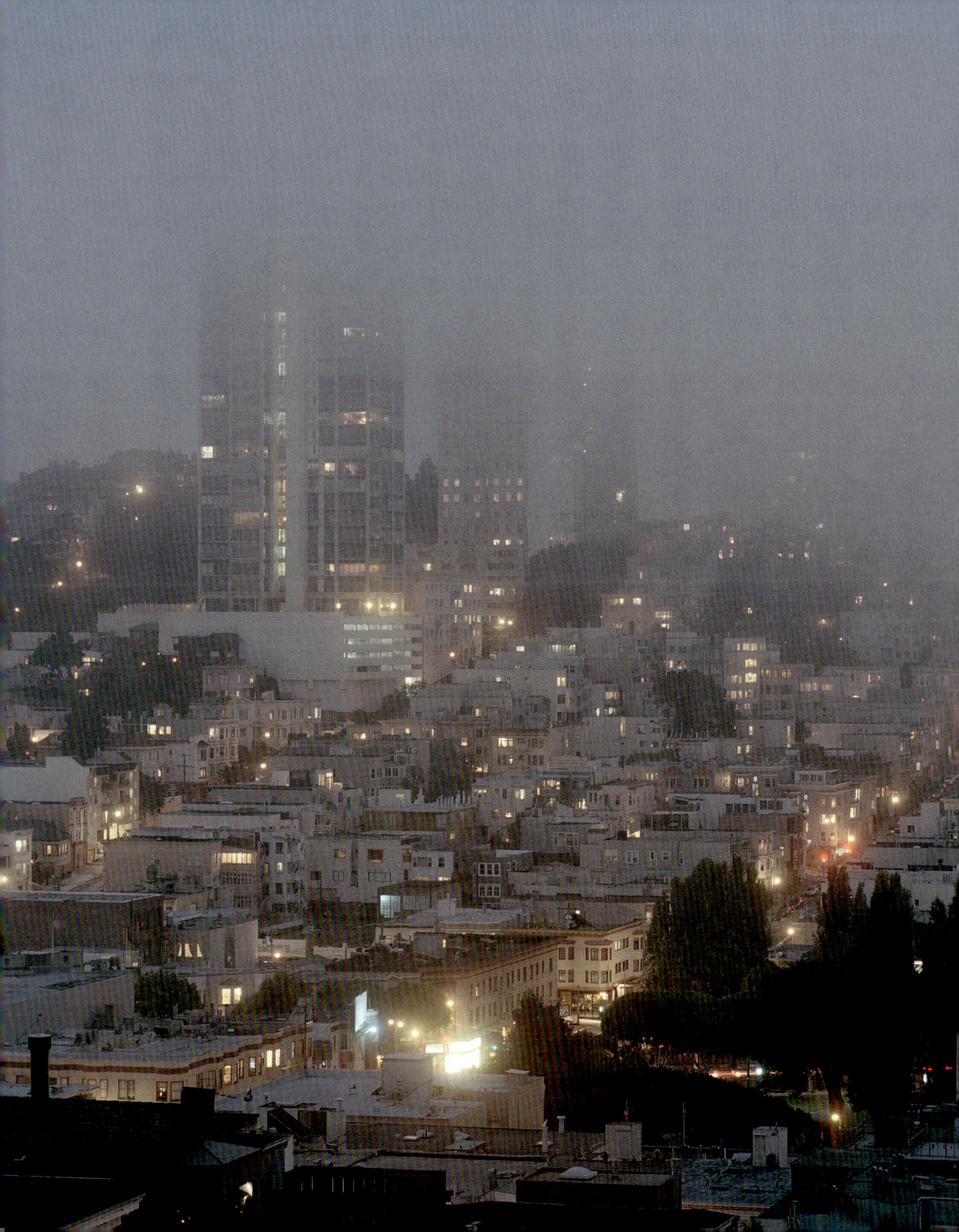

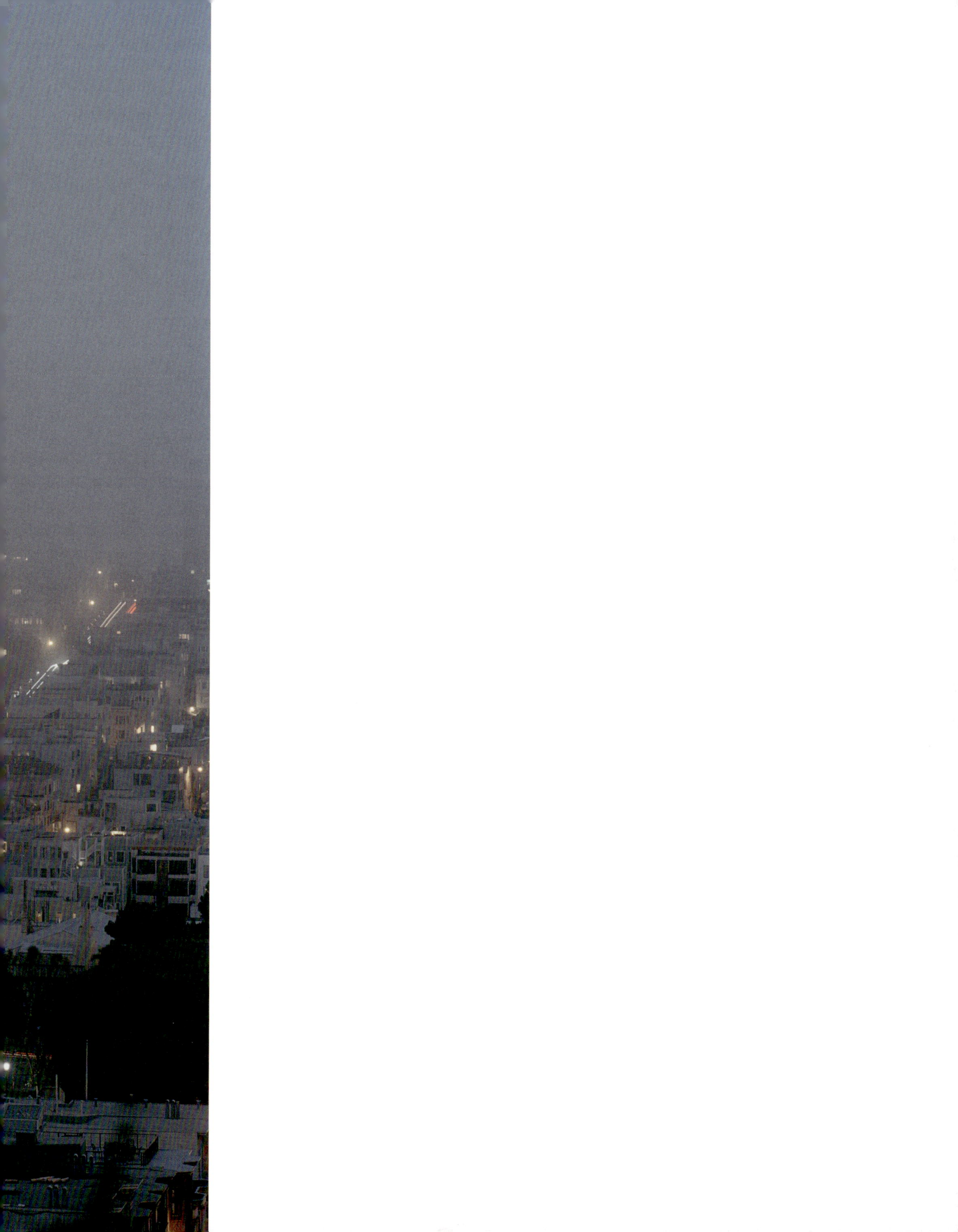

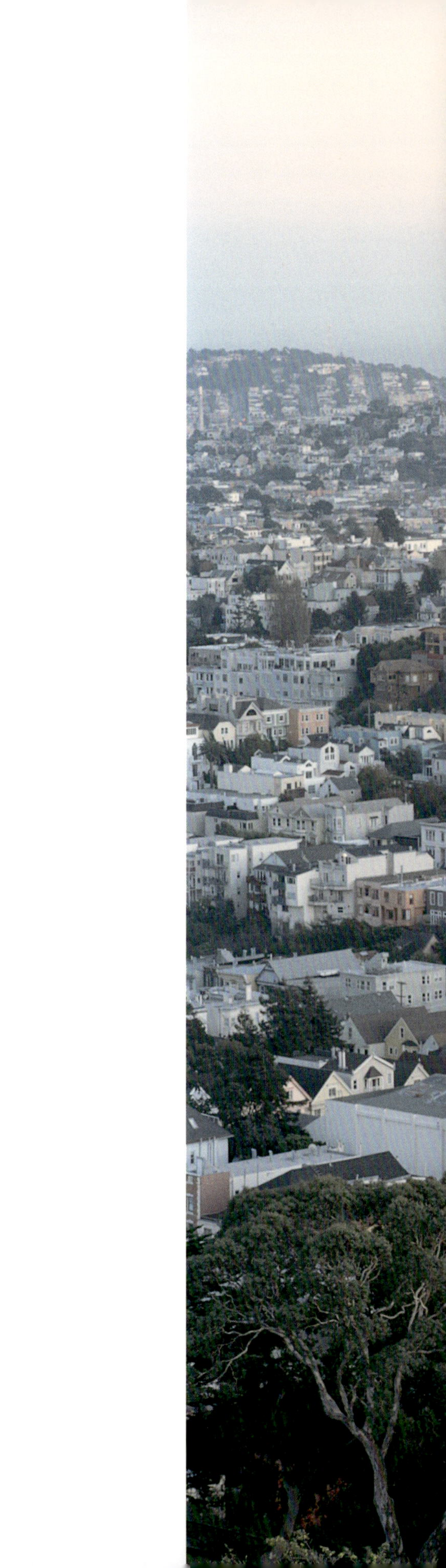

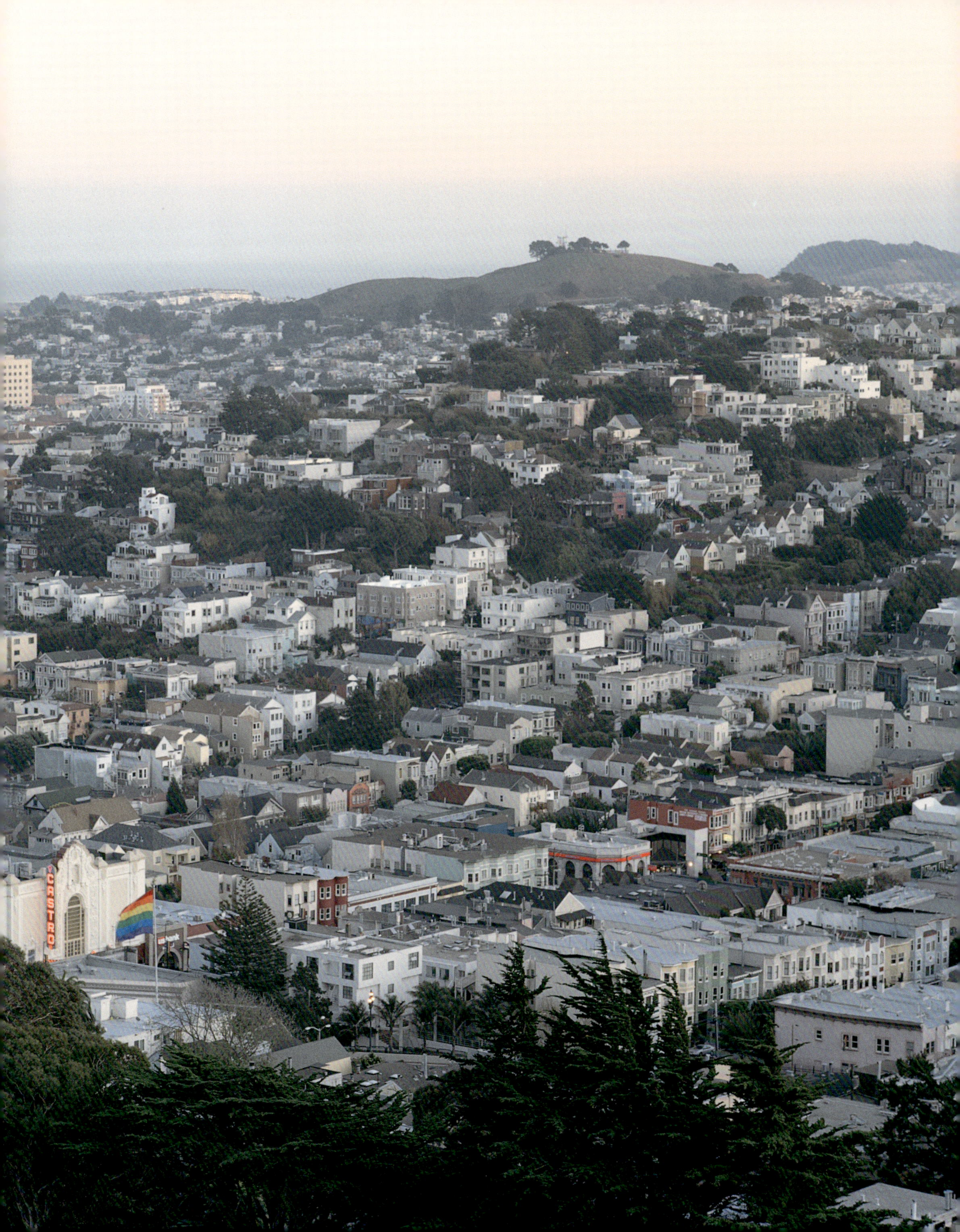
CASTRO

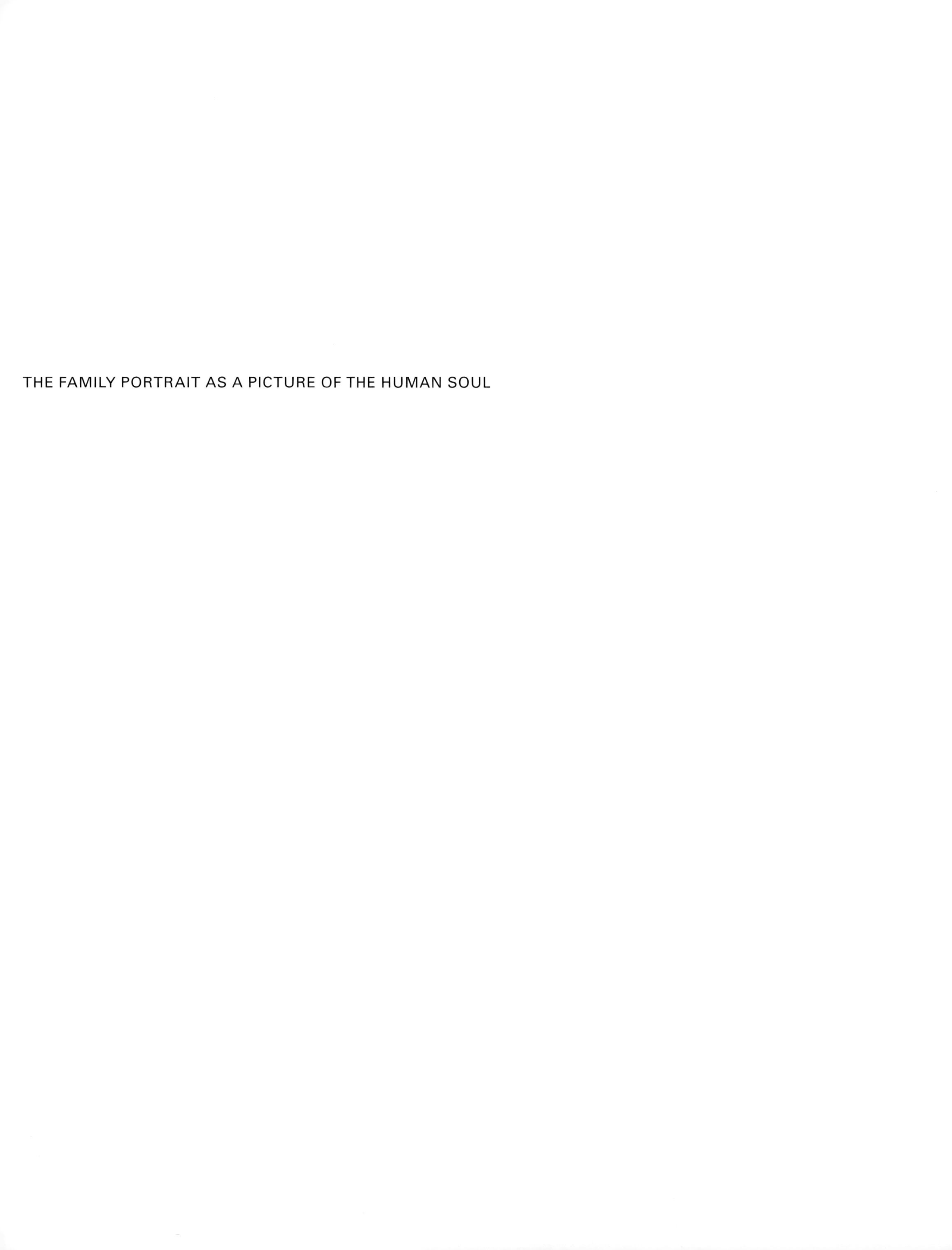

THE FAMILY PORTRAIT AS A PICTURE OF THE HUMAN SOUL

»The people in the audience looked at the pictures, and the people in the pictures looked back at them. They recognized each other. A Japanese poet has said that, when you look into a mirror, you do not see your reflection, your reflection sees you.« [Edward Steichen]——Our family is the mirror of our life. From it, we inherit not just our genetic predisposition but also modes of behavior that have inscribed themselves over generations. These behavioral modes include gestures and facial expressions, eating and sleeping habits, patterns of relationships and communication, and much more besides. For our present and future, our family offers an interpretative model for our feelings and perceptions.——When looking at family photos, we can ask ourselves many questions. For example: where are the parents standing, and are they standing together or apart? To what extent are the parents connecting with the children? Are they capable of doing so? And if yes, are they doing so freely and openly, in a way that gives the child a sense of security? Or in a dutiful or clinging fashion, in which the security is provided by the child? Such things may all be legible in family portraits and are used in psychology to discover where the nucleus of a person's family lies, and to arrive at explanations for their patterns of behavior. This can prove a revelation, an inner liberation that enables us to choose whether we want to maintain long-held attitudes or would rather throw them overboard.——We all have eyes that make us fundamentally capable of seeing. If we trust ourselves to ask the right questions, we can uncover the information that is concealed within images. In most cases this requires a very thorough and detailed description of the picture, which, when spoken out loud, allows us to understand, in a fully conscious way, what we are looking at. In this way we can decode paintings and photographs.——Daniel Schumann has concentrated on the themes of »Death« and »Family« since the very beginning of his artistic career. For his project *Purpur Braun Grau Weiß Schwarz* [2009], he accompanied, in a series of photographic portraits, dying residents of a hospice in which he had previously completed his alternative civilian service. The photographer devoted his next project, *Elisabeth und Wilhelm* [2010], to his grandmother Elisabeth, who had died suddenly while he was away travelling, so that he did not have the opportunity to say goodbye to her properly.——The resulting book opens with a series of pictures of Elisabeth's husband Wilhelm, suffering from dementia. The way in which Daniel Schumann represents his grandfather establishes a link between the two projects: the individuals photographed in *Purpur Braun Grau Weiß Schwarz*, and Wilhelm in *Elisabeth und Wilhelm*, are portrayed with great dignity. They appear contemplative, as if in transition towards a very different world.—After his paternal family of origin, Daniel Schumann chose, as the subject of his diploma dissertation, families with a child with a life-threatening illness in their midst. He embarked on this project in 2009 and continues to pursue it at intervals right up to the present. The families he has photographed include those with several children, single parents, and families of other nationalities who are living in Germany or who have already become German citizens. Many of these family portraits leave an indelible impression. In some, the burden that the family must carry makes itself felt at the formal level.—Why, in this third series, Daniel Schumann should again tackle the subject of »Death and Dying,« is an interesting question and one that remains to be answered. In seeking out his subjects, the photographer's focus is particularly drawn to families. For his latest project, *International Orange*, he travels to San Francisco with the support of a Fulbright scholarship, and photographs gay and lesbian couples and families. Despite all the repression to which these individuals may have been exposed during their own childhoods, depending on what part of the country they come from or to which ethnic or religious group they belong, the majority seem very happy.—Just as the aspiring middle classes in the nineteenth century used photography to proudly document their financial independence, these homosexual couples and families likewise seem to welcome the medium as an opportunity to show the world that they, too, can now participate in all aspects of life in a self-determined way. A decisive social shift thus also becomes apparent through these photographs.—Alongside the single parents to whom we have already become accustomed amongst heterosexuals, above all in our towns and cities, the viewer is also presented with constellations that are still unusual: two mothers, two fathers, or single homosexual parents with one or several natural or adopted children. The staging of the photographs is thereby directed by the sitters, as Daniel Schumann wanted to allow his subjects the greatest possible freedom to determine the way in which they present themselves. In the individuality of the resulting pictures, they come across as middle-class families who are having their photo taken for friends or relatives. The poses, decors and/or the choice of location thereby reveal much about the tastes, attitudes and origins of the people we are looking at. The many-sided nature of family bonds is reflected in the diversity of these photographic portraits. The new family groups – however unfamiliar they may still appear to some – represent an addition and a complement to our modern social structure. What these families, in their various possible combinations, signify for the legibility of family portraits is something that pyschology and sociology will have to answer.—For Daniel Schumann, the choice of his subjects is invariably also a personal search. He began studying death early in his life. Death and love, as the foundations of the family, are recurrent themes in literature, opera, pictures and art as a whole. It is noticeable that Daniel Schumann pays great attention to the changes that these life events bring with them in our modern world, and in so doing places the element of today in tomorrow under the magnifying glass, or more accurately beneath his lens. For death is no longer really part of our lives. Partly because increased life expectancy has made death less of an everyday presence, and partly because we bracket it out of our existence and leave it to professionals like doctors and carers in hospitals and hospices. The fact that Daniel Schumann addresses love in all its forms shows his interest in its possibilities and is at the same time his plea for freedom and openness in our society. Love and death: two realities that the young artist confronts.——The photographs by Daniel Schumann go far beyond mere documentation. They are infinitely more. In the first instance they are pictures of his way of seeing, which always contains other ways of seeing, too. They are personal and social souvenirs that we like to call our memory. They are containers of experience and experiences, and as such they illustrate how our existence in the world is changing. They are a language for which we have yet to find the words.——If all were able to understand otherness not as an attack on our existence but as a broadening of our individual potential and personal outlook, we would go through life richer. There is fear attached. But opening up to alternative ways of living makes us fulfilled and happy, and the fear evaporates – sometimes. Daniel Schumann parades this opportunity very clearly before us. Let's take it!

Christina Leber DZ Bank Art Collection

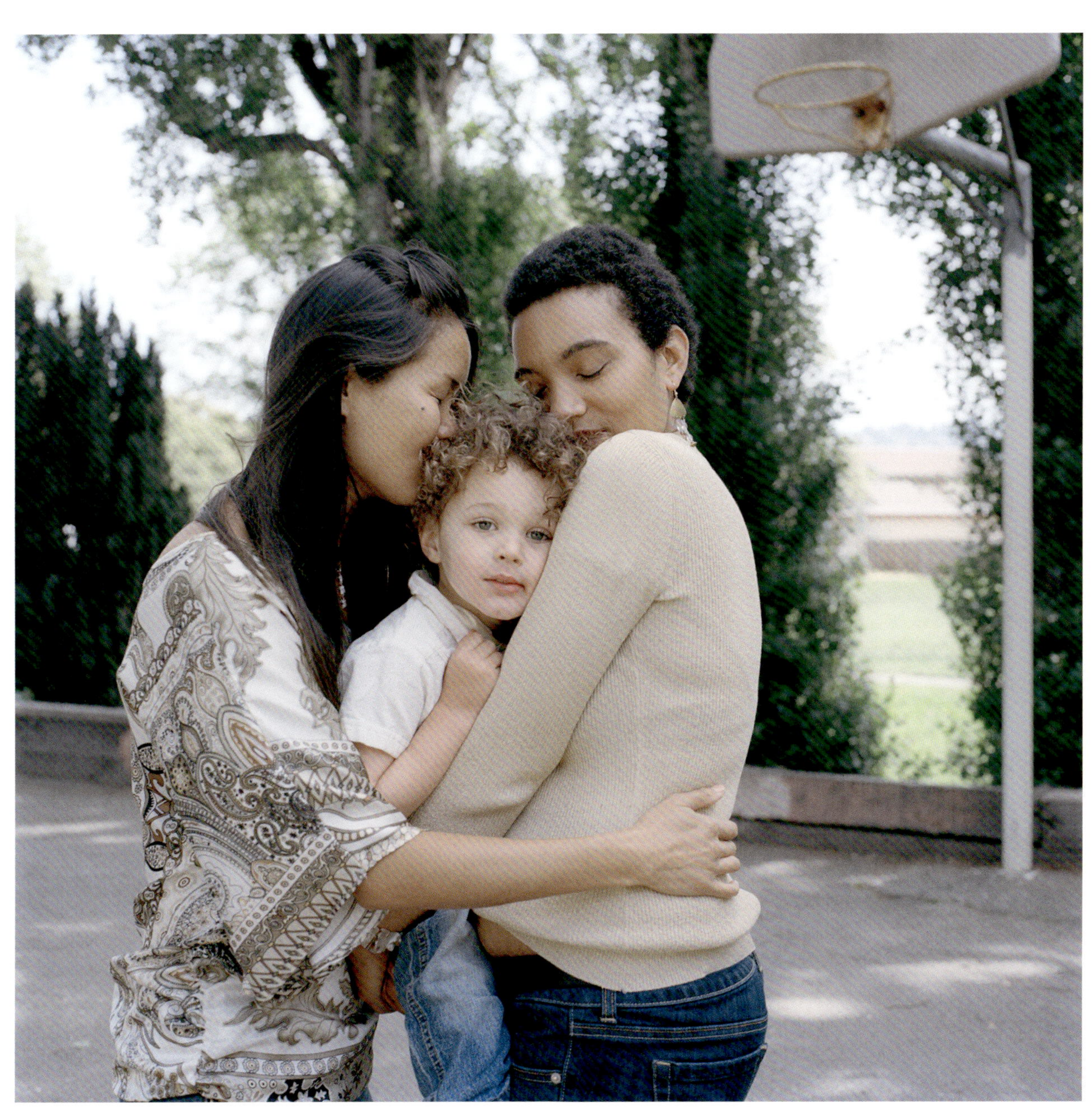

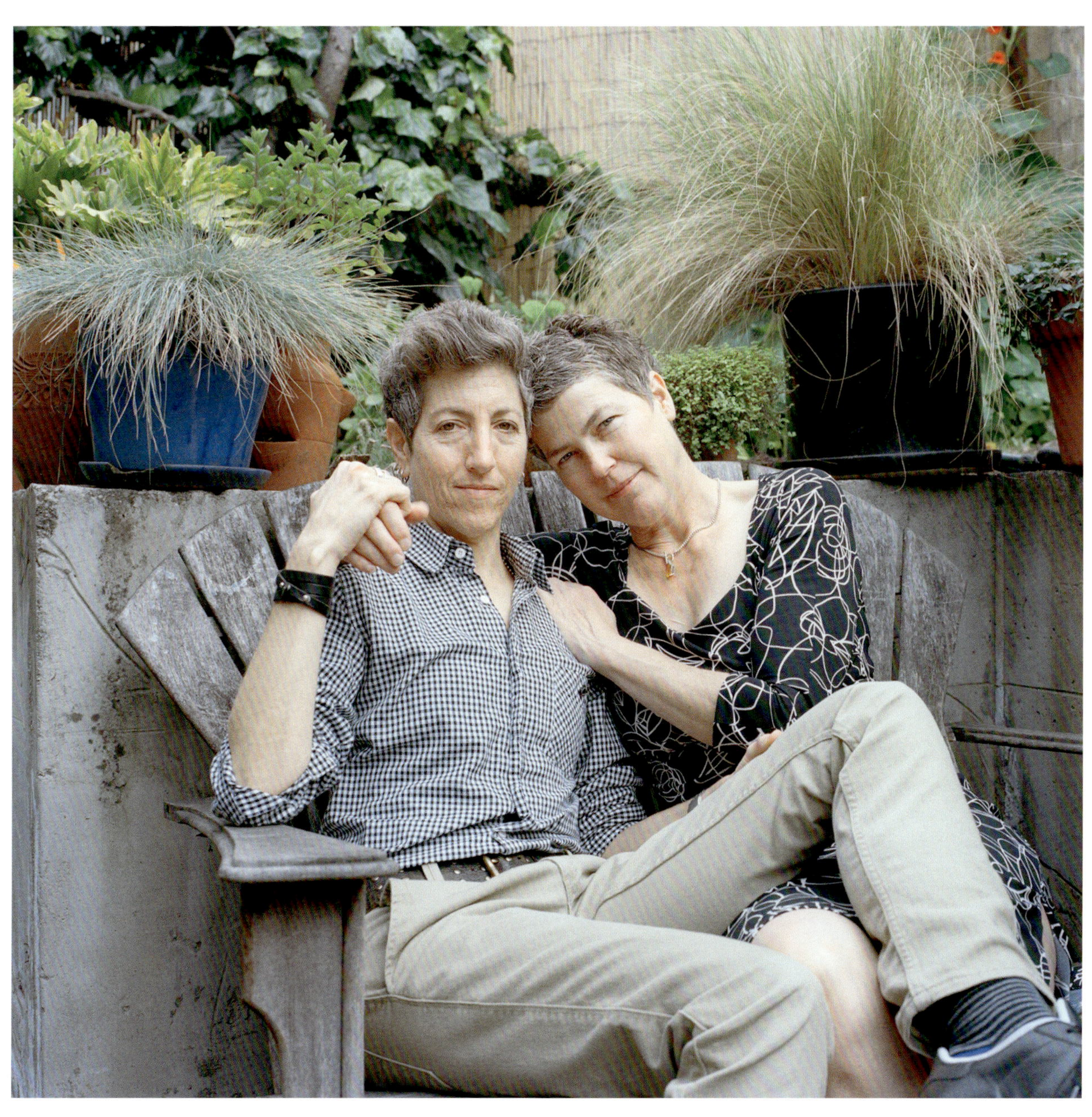

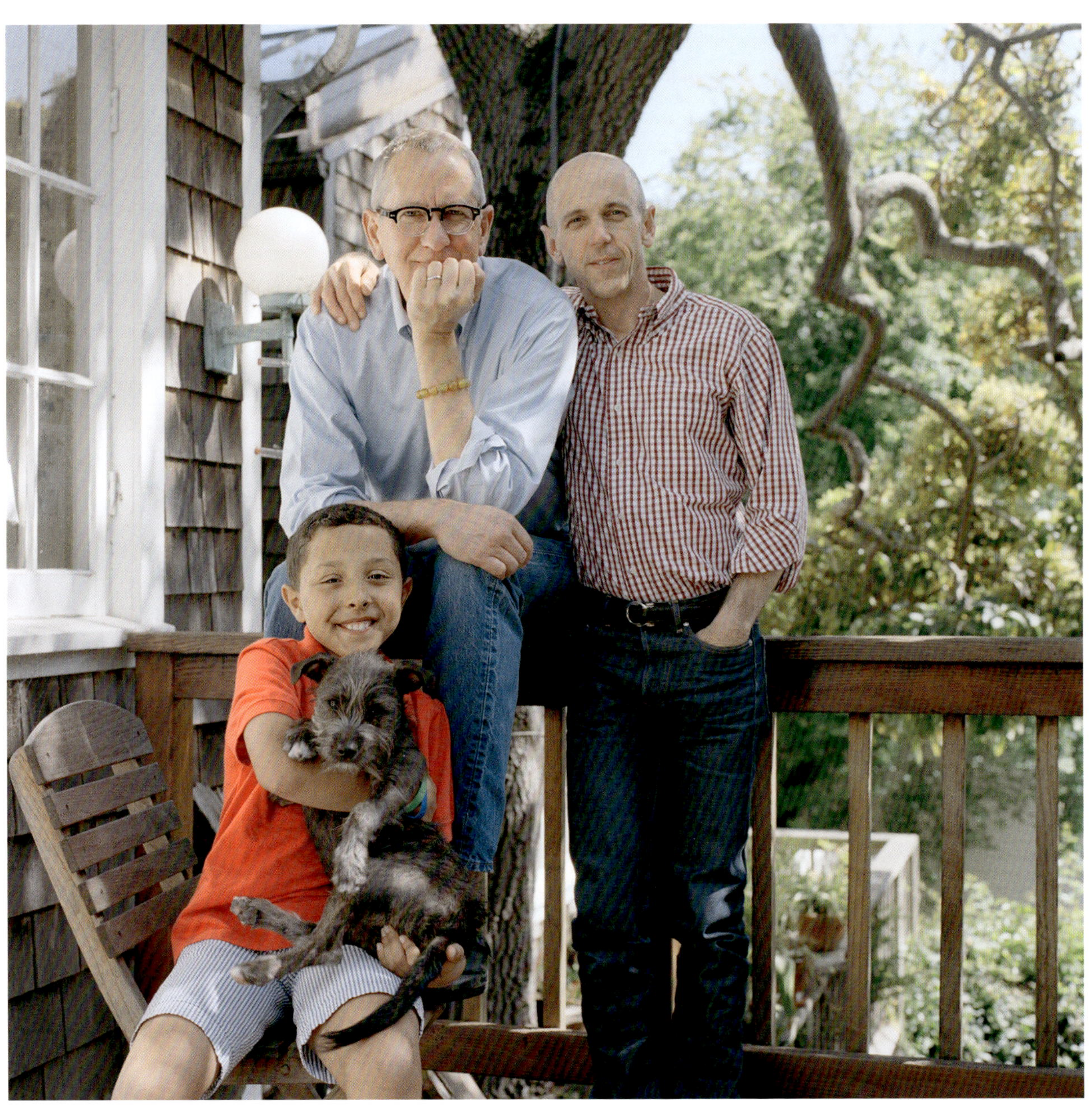

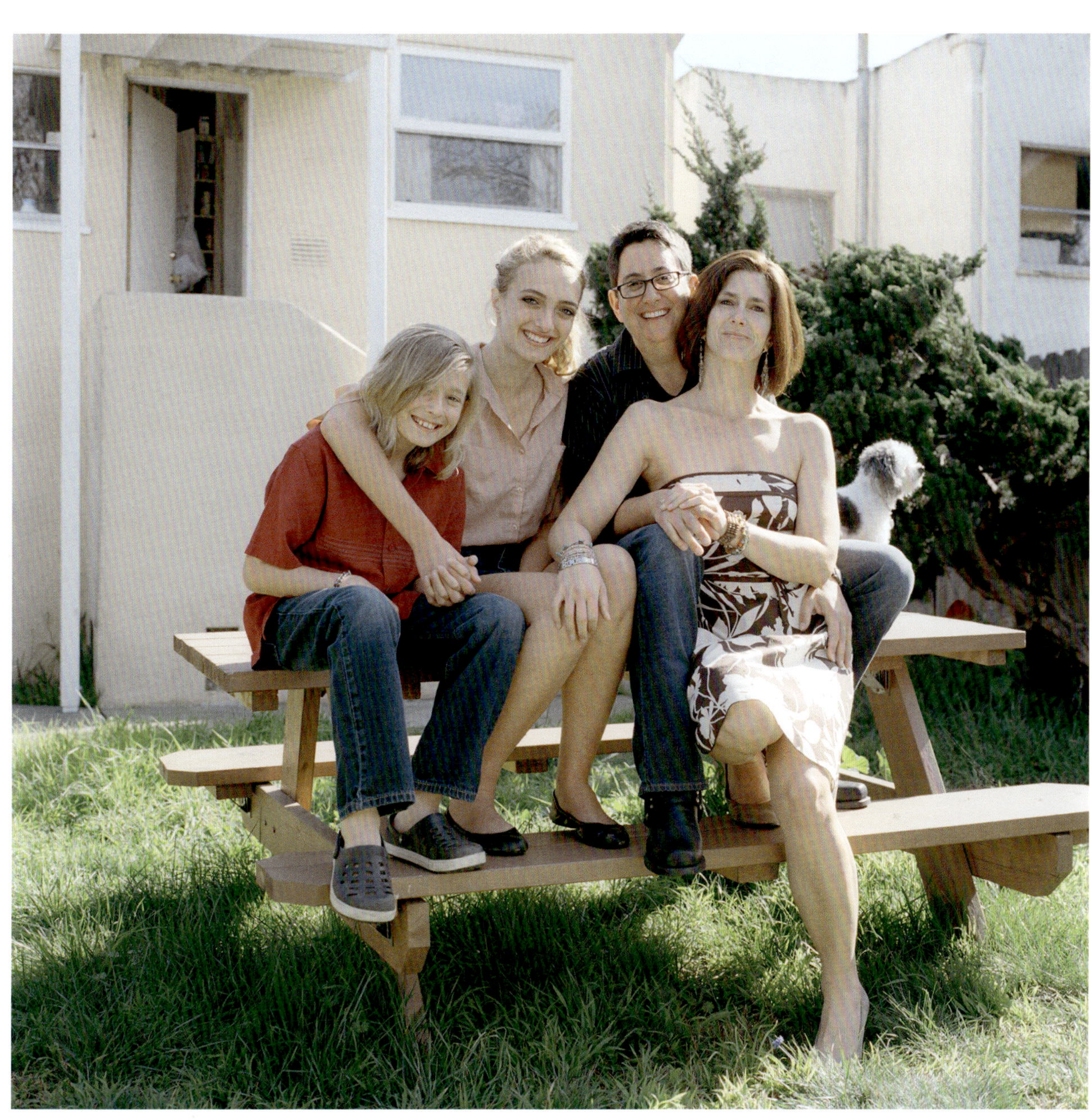

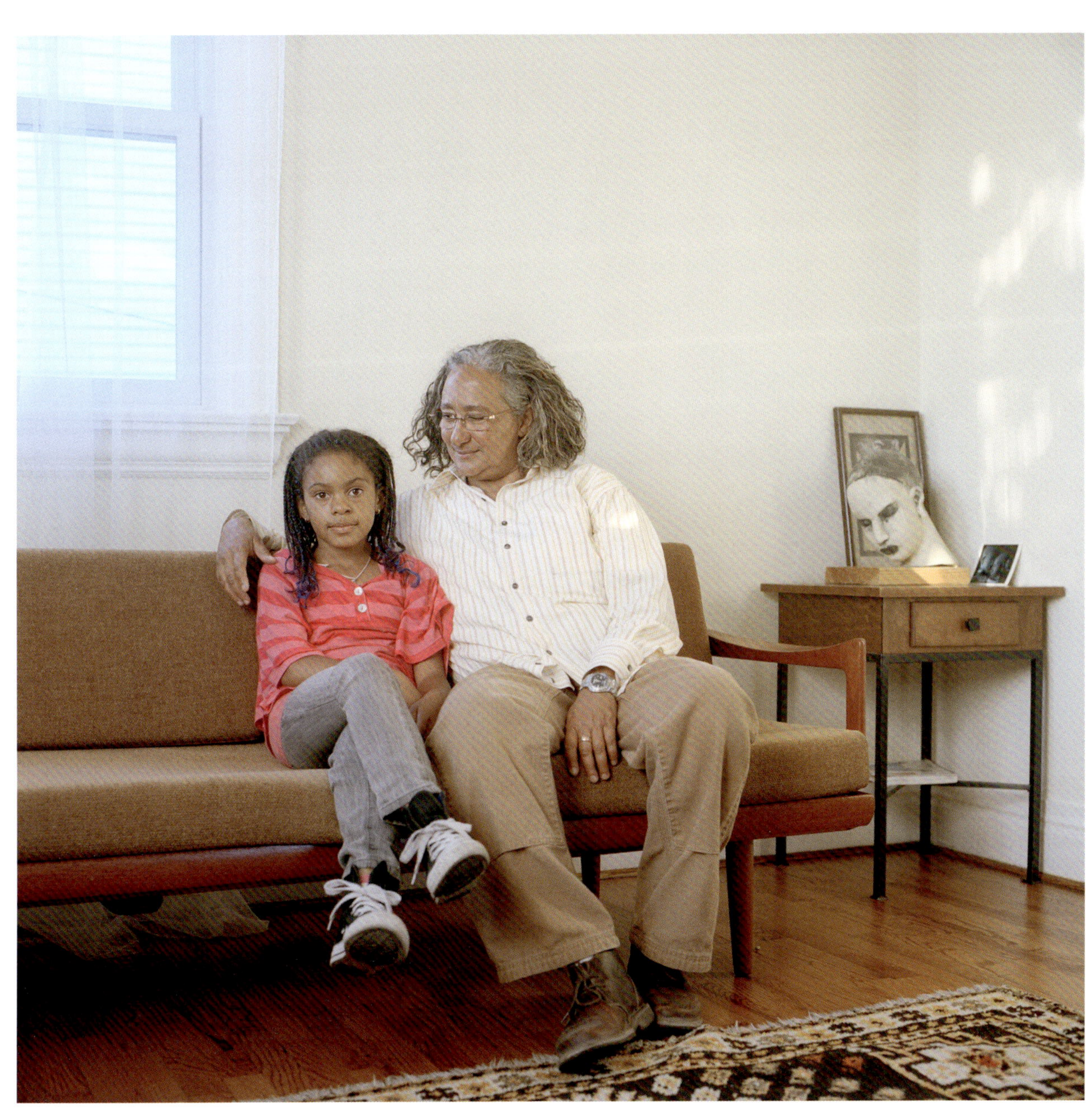

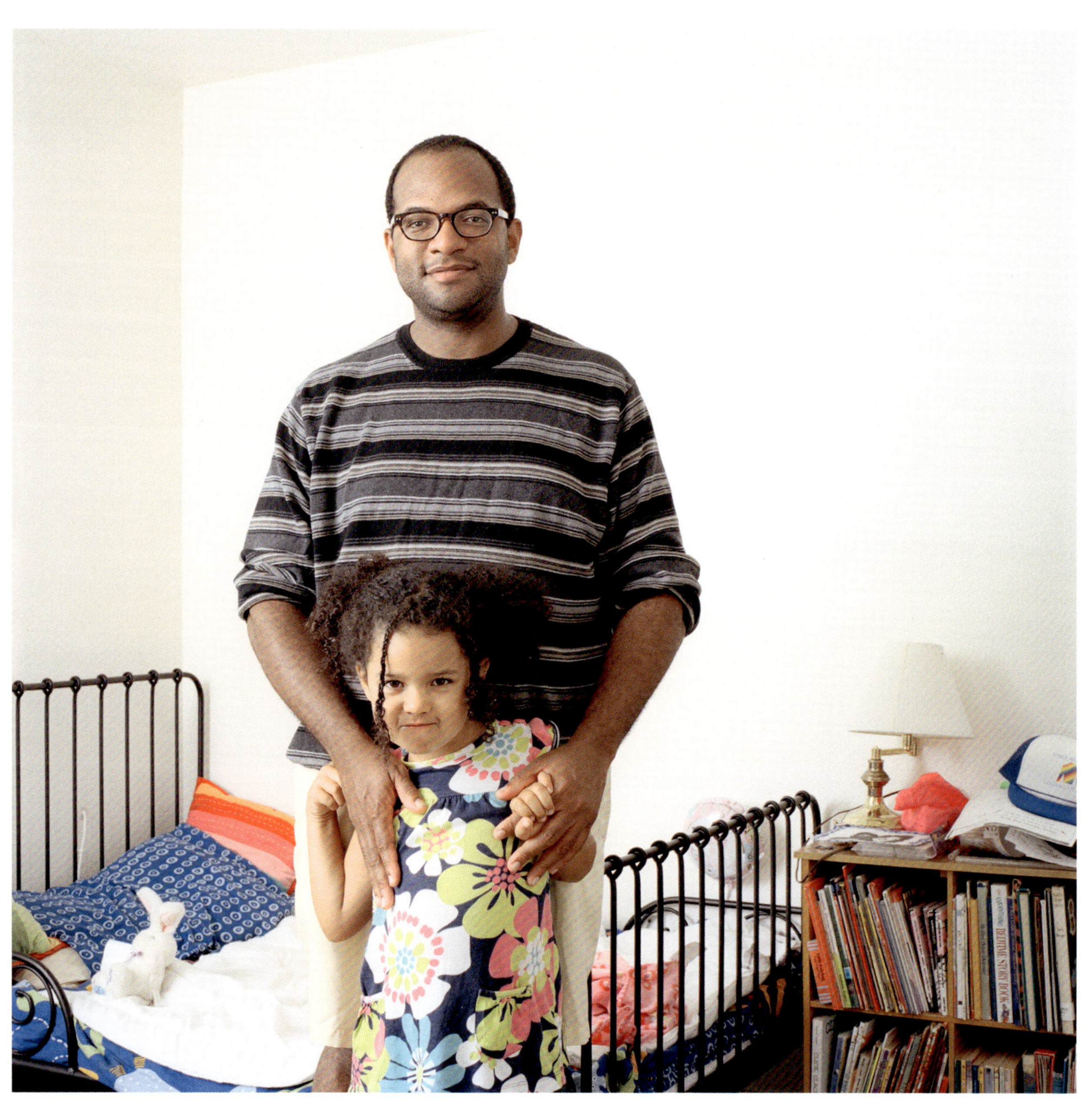

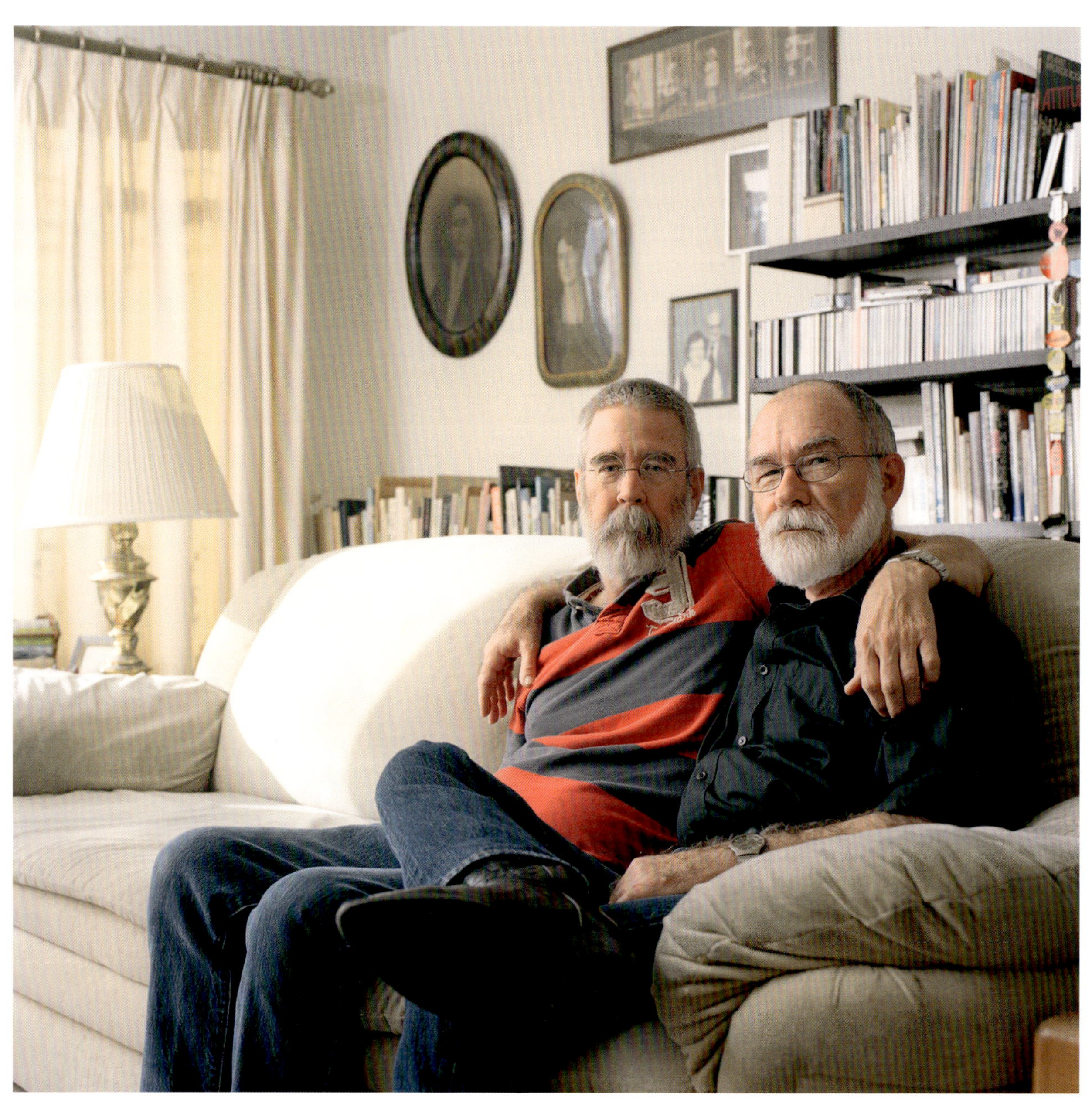

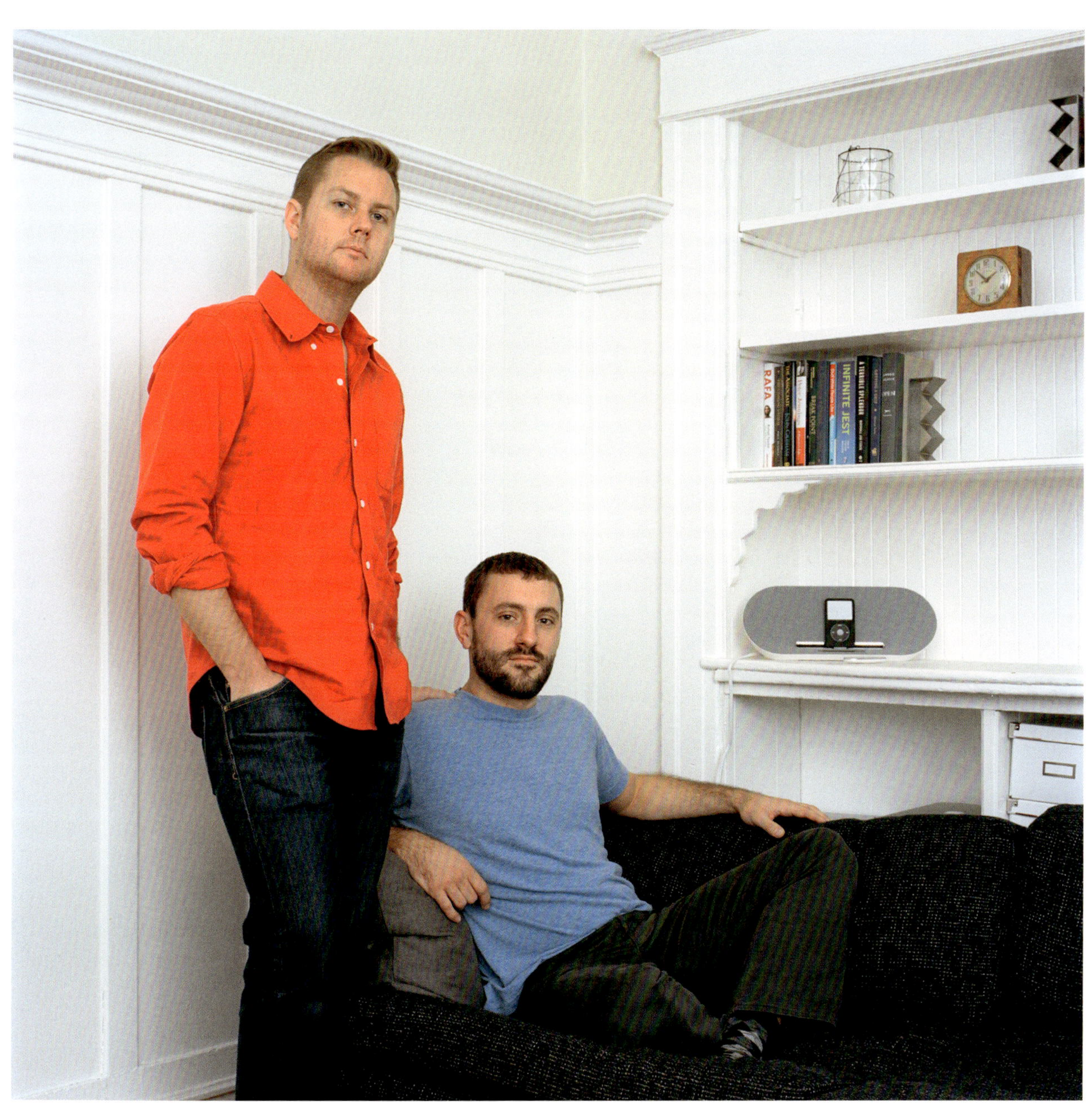
RAFA
BREAK POINT
INFINITE JEST
A TERRIBLE SPLENDOR

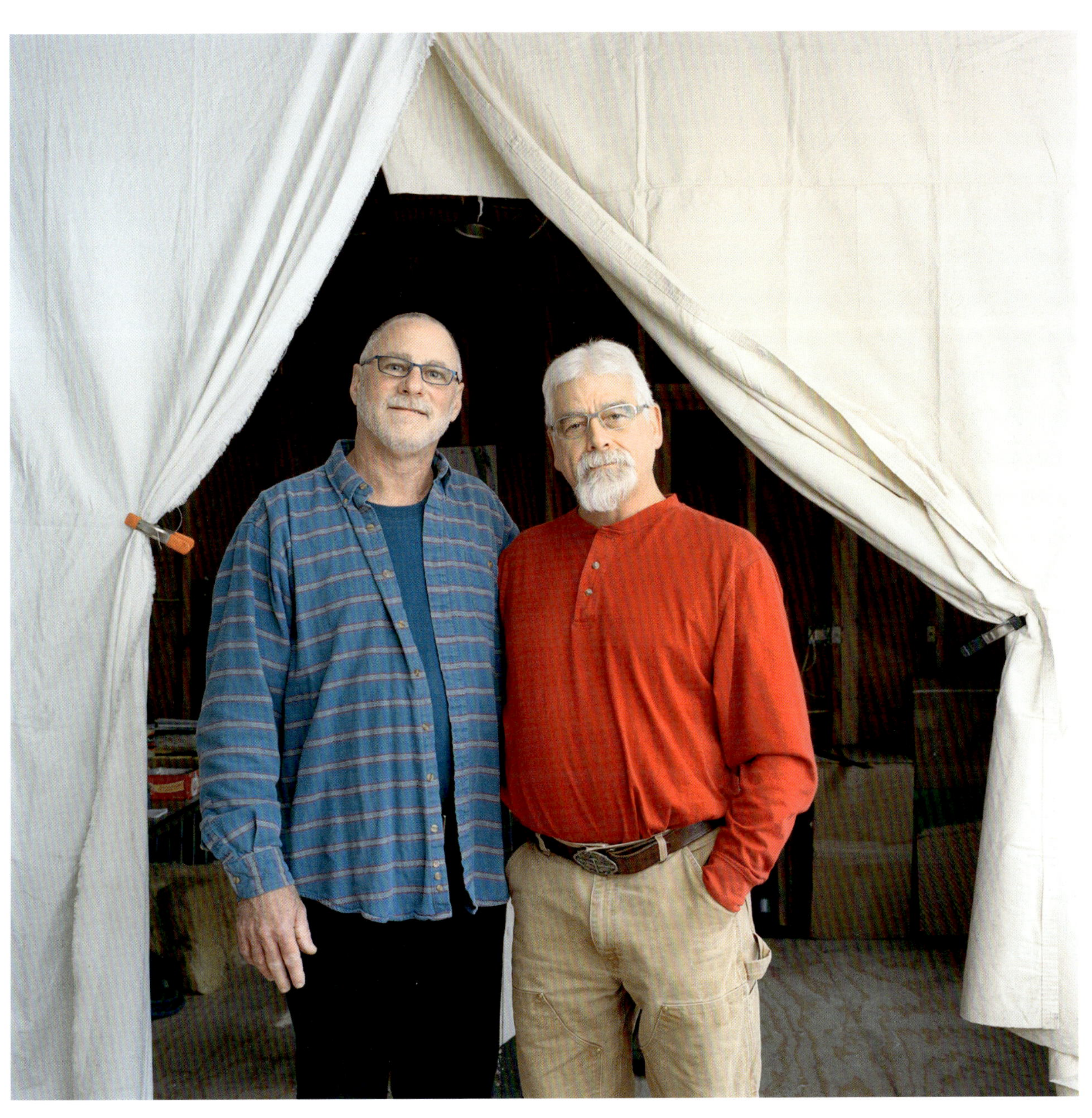

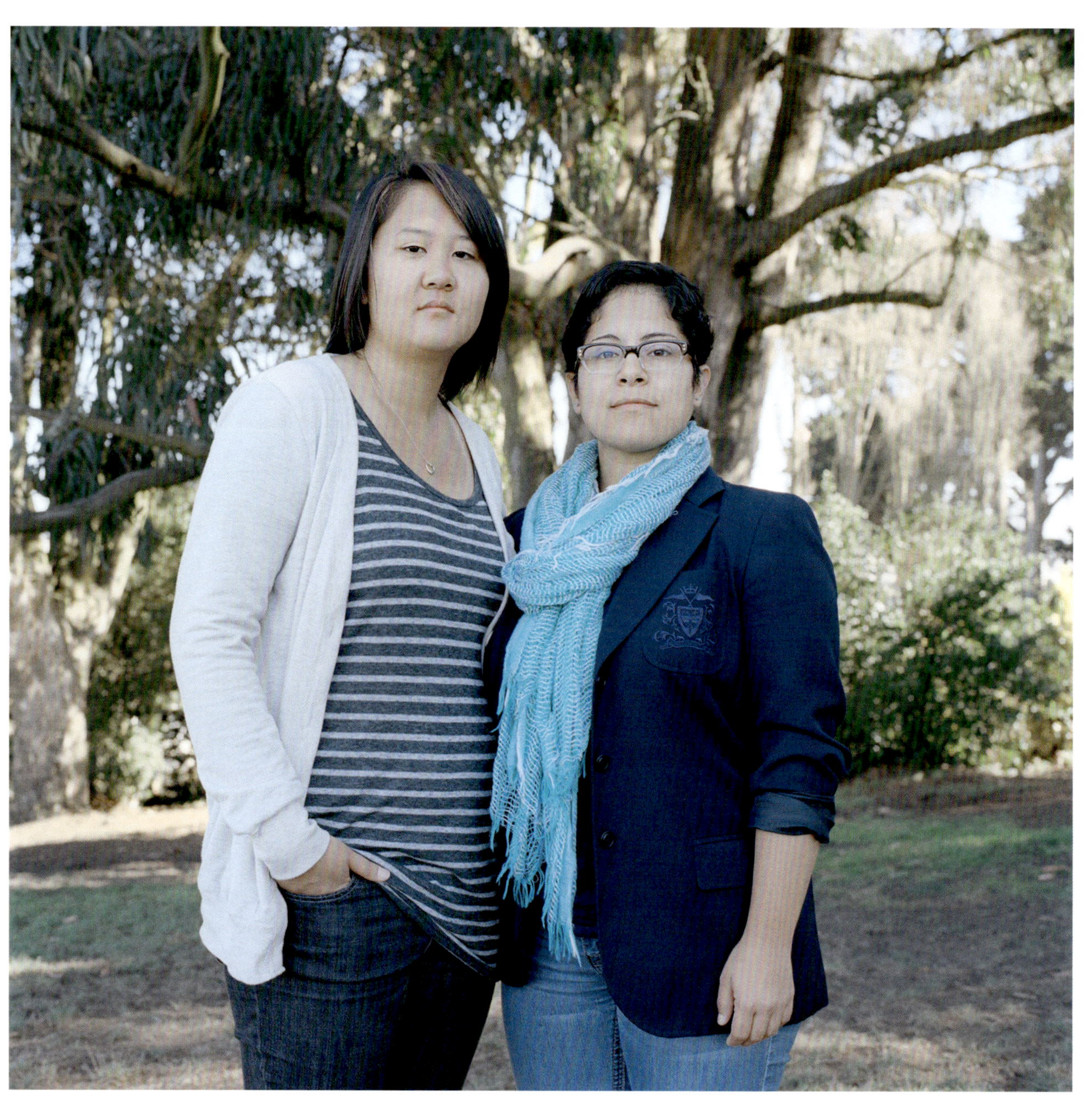

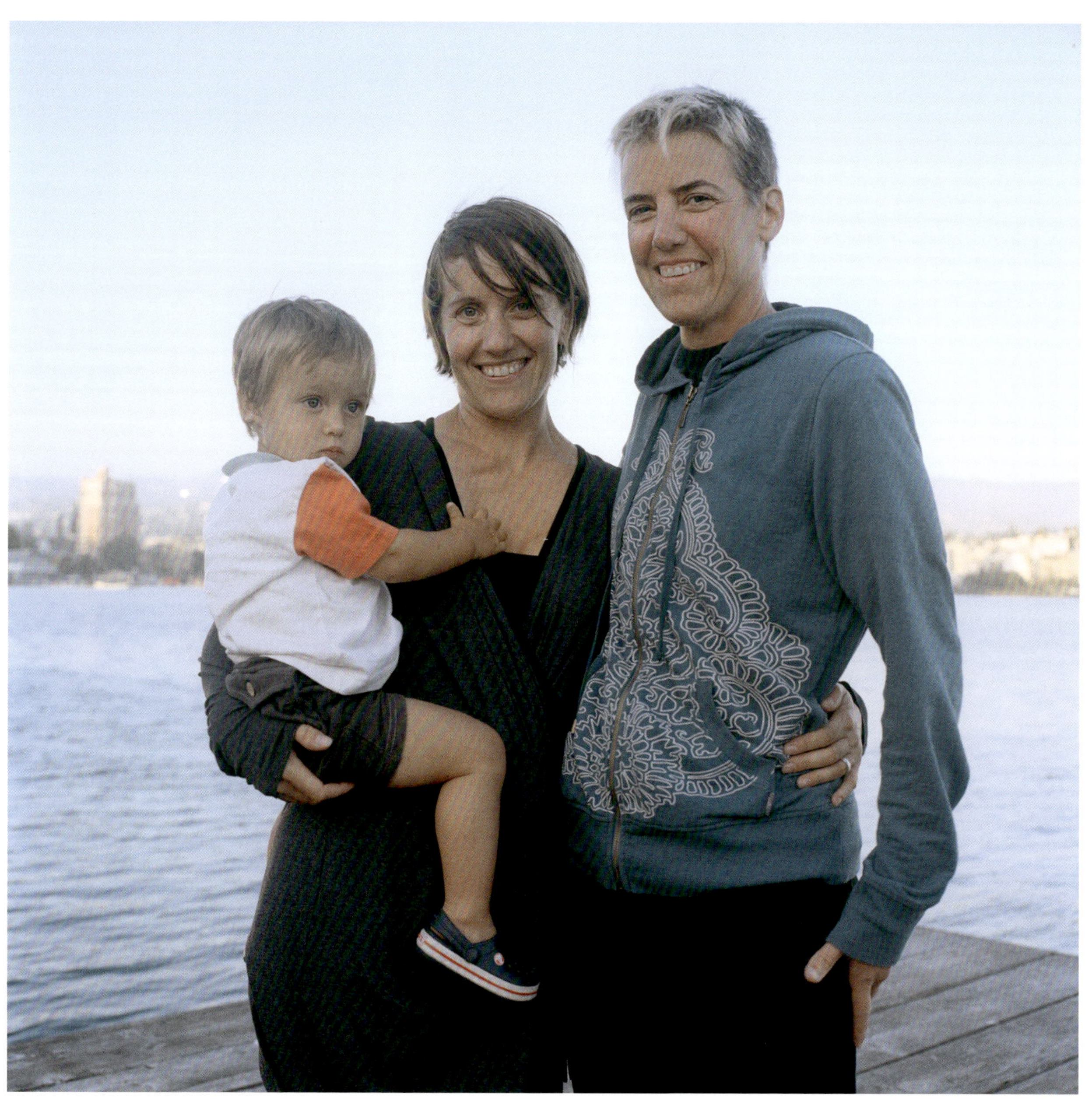

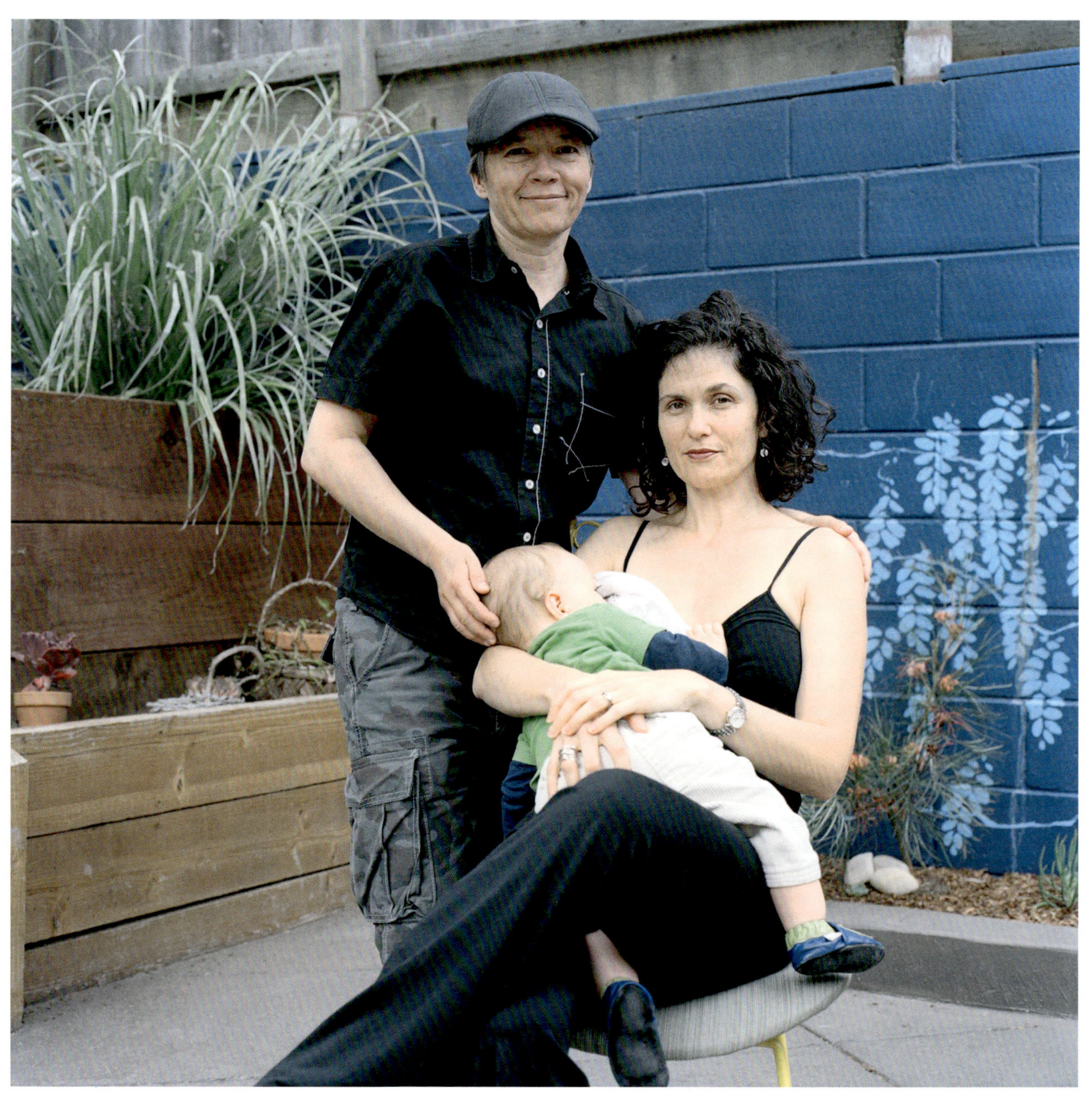

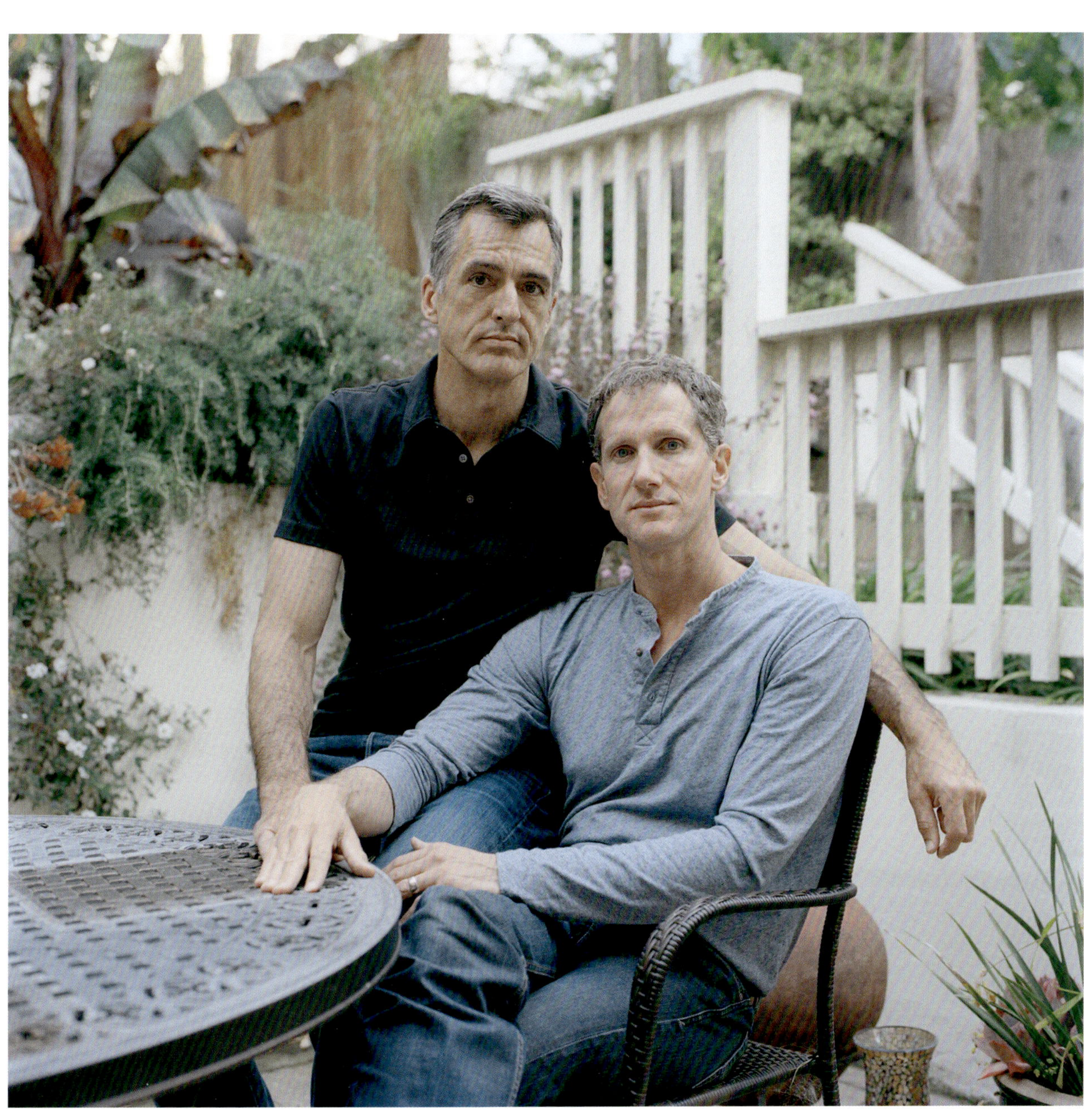

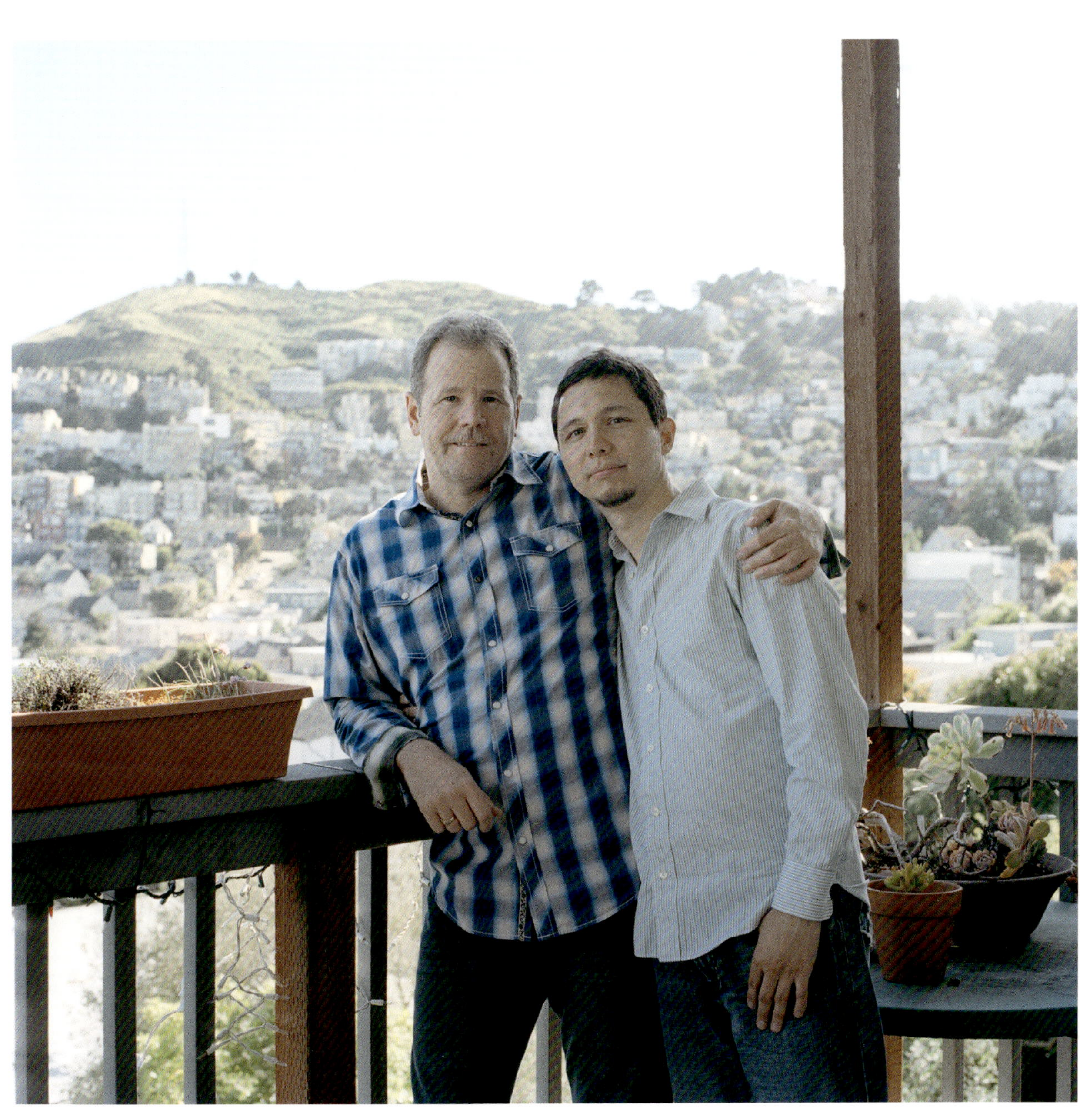

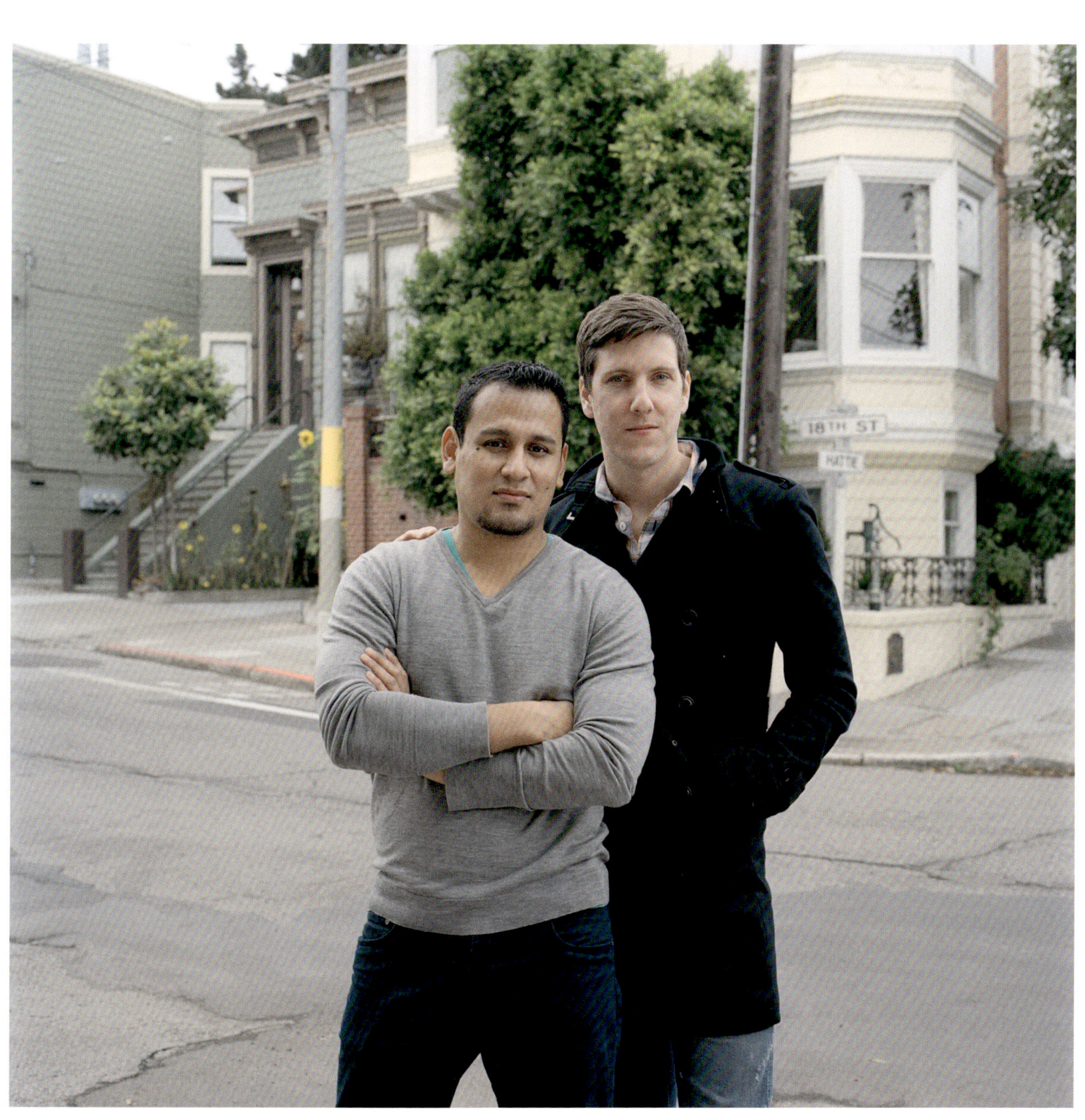
18TH ST

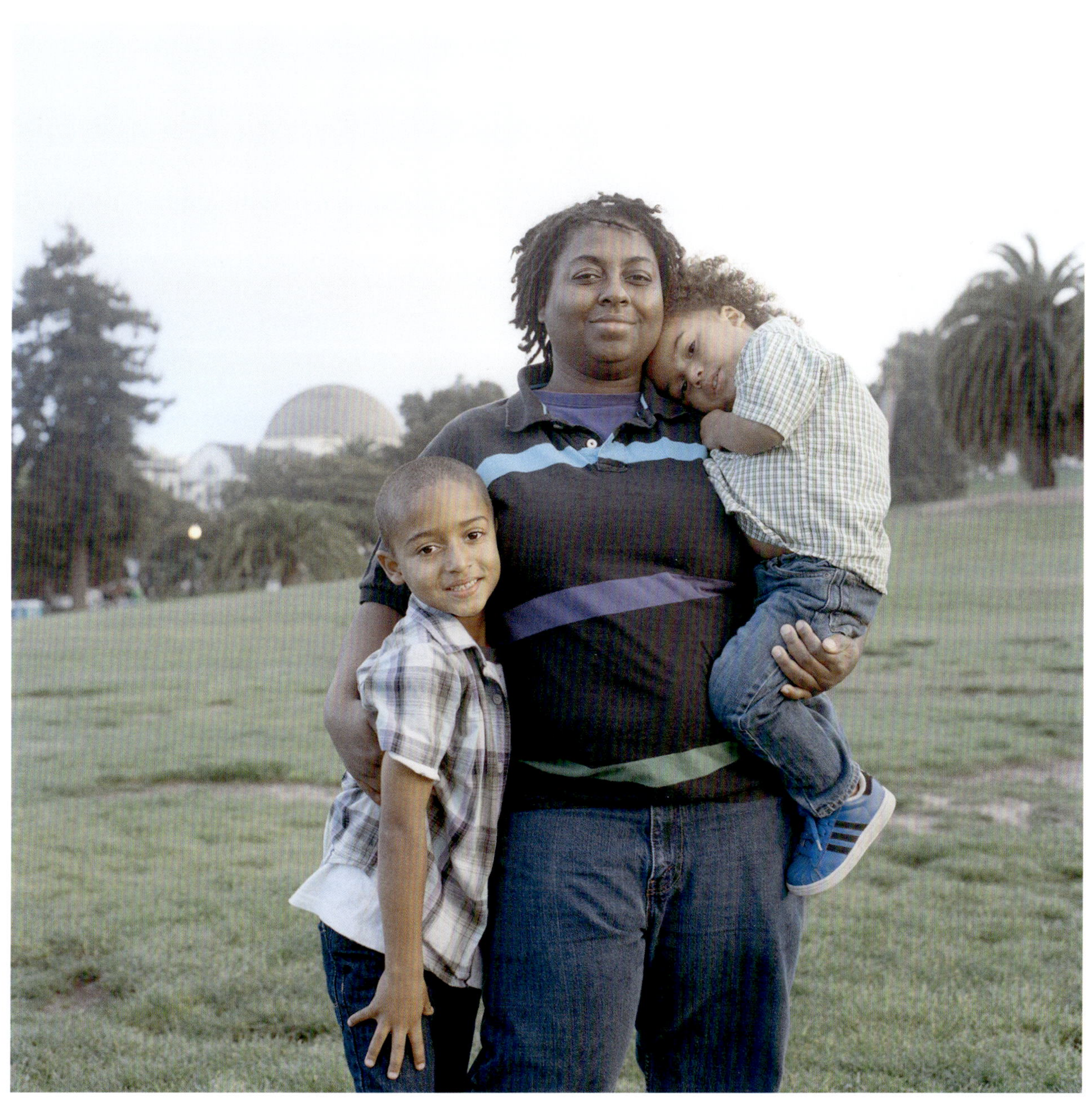

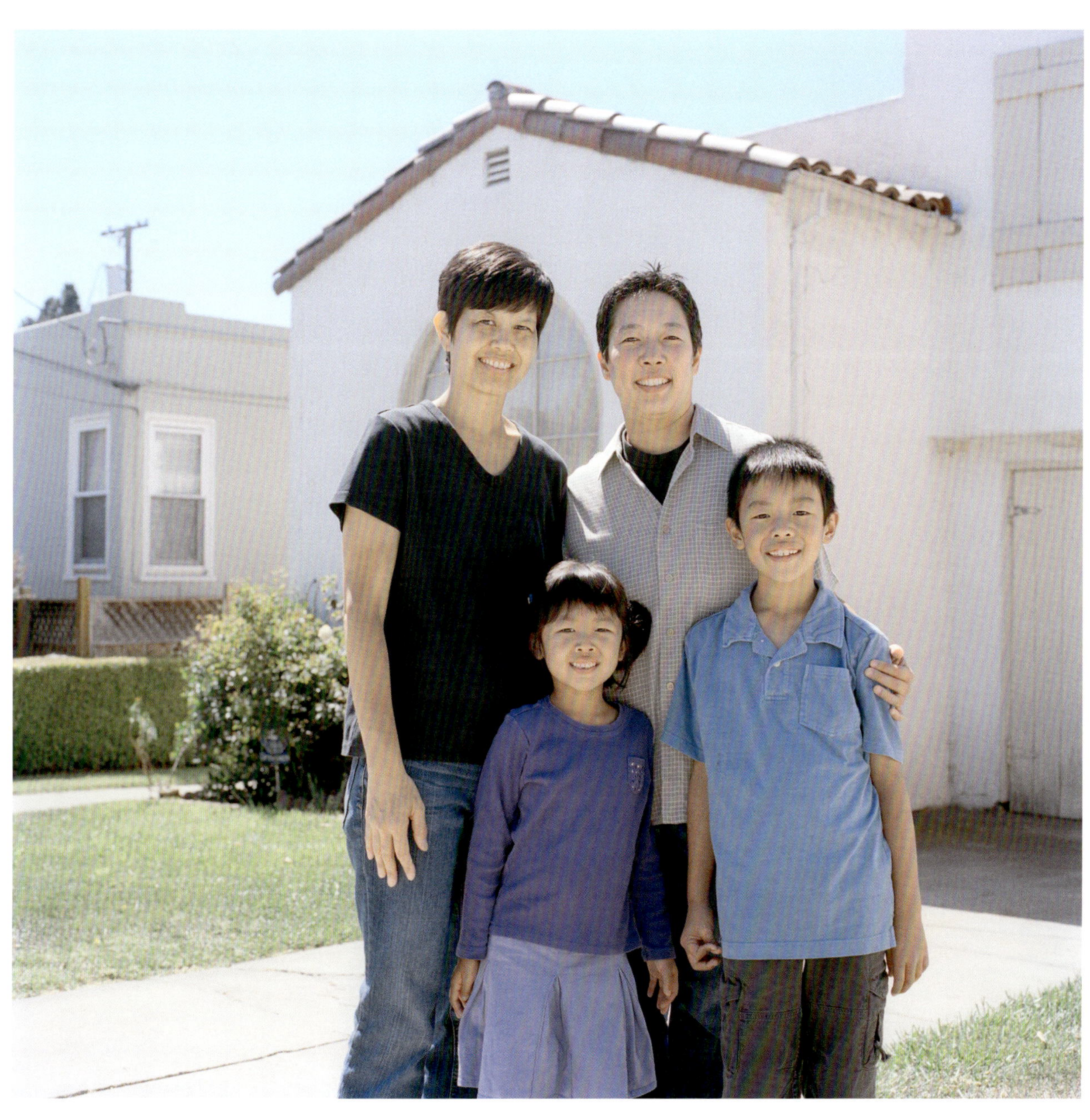

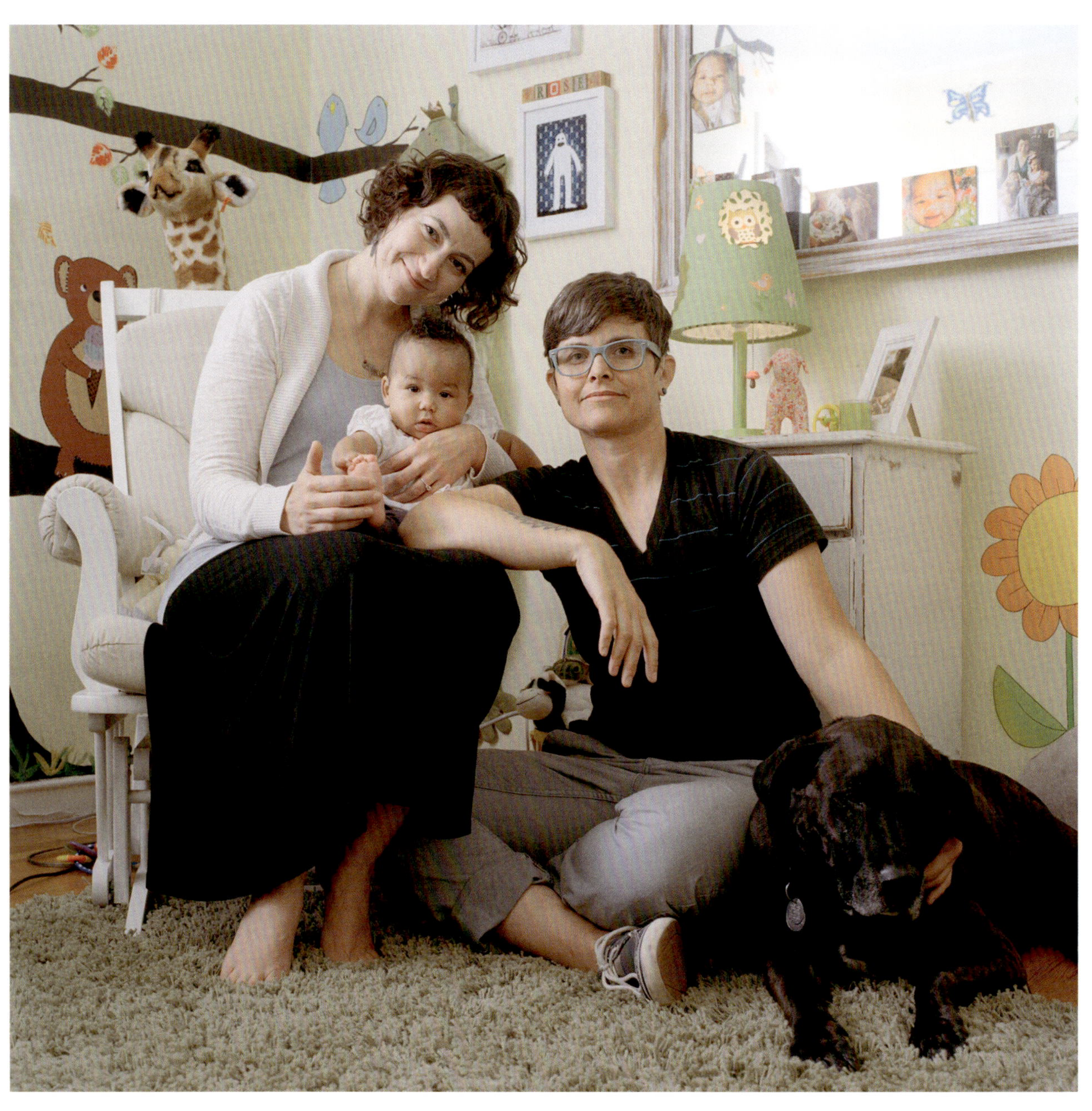

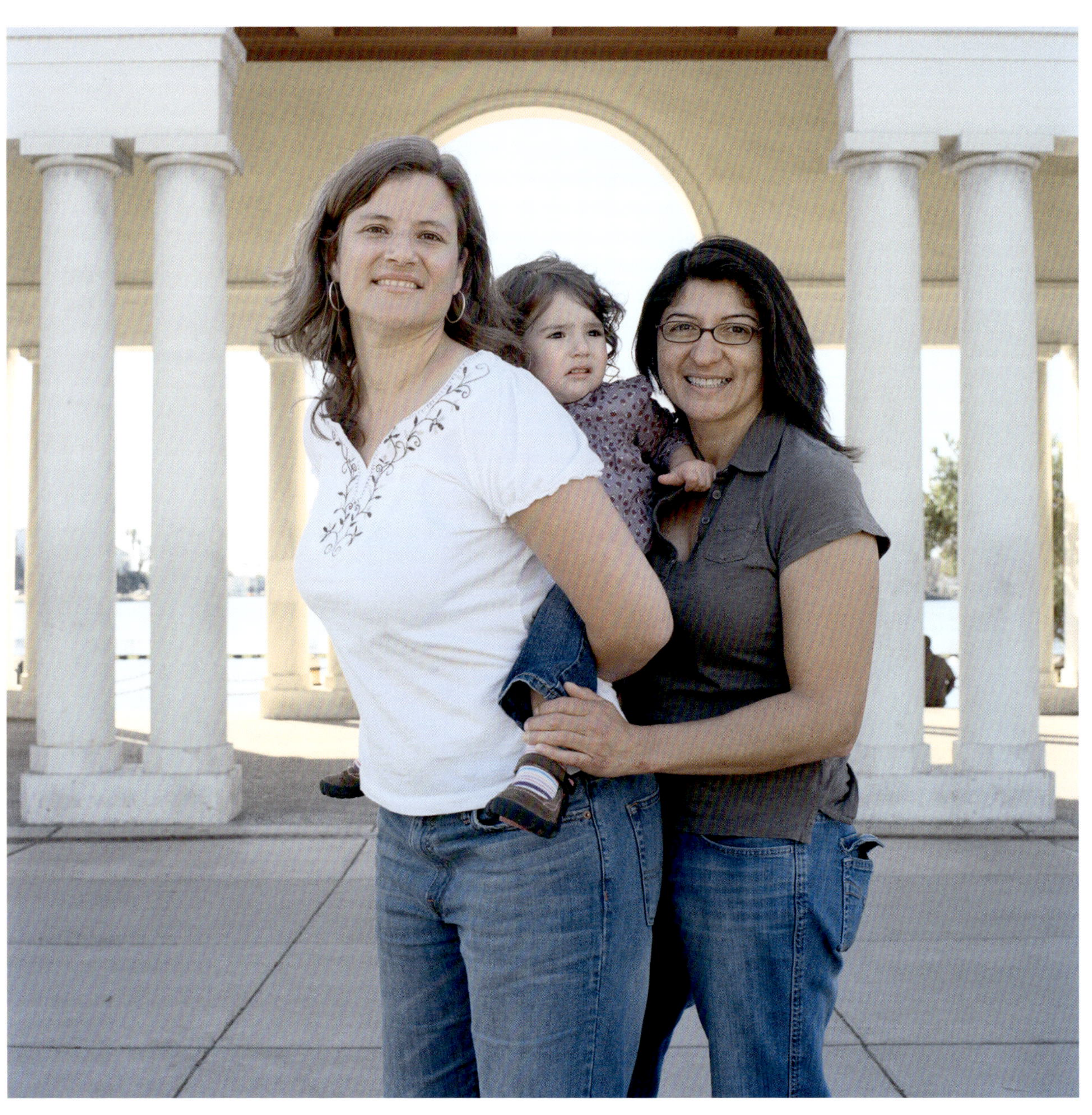

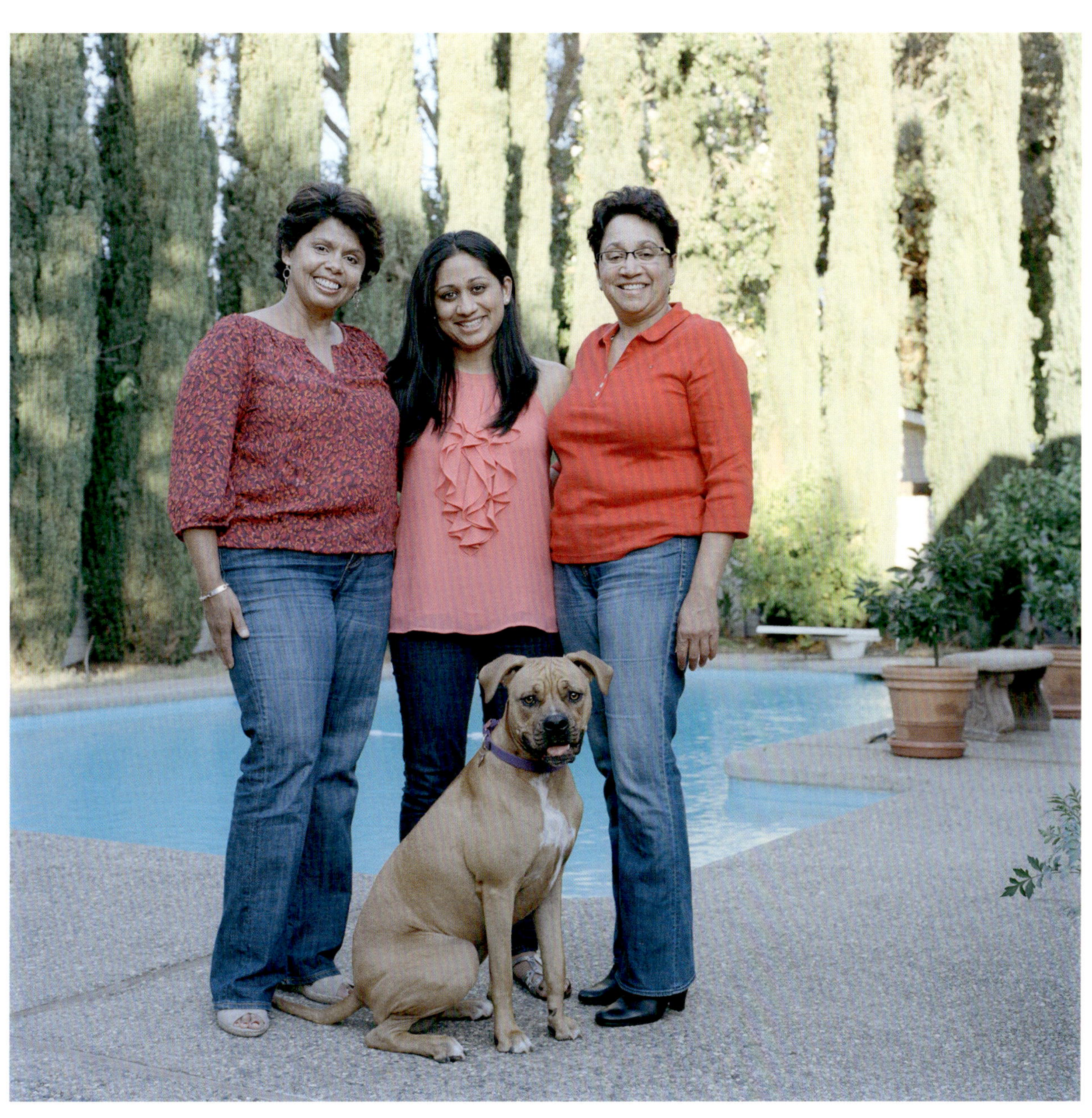

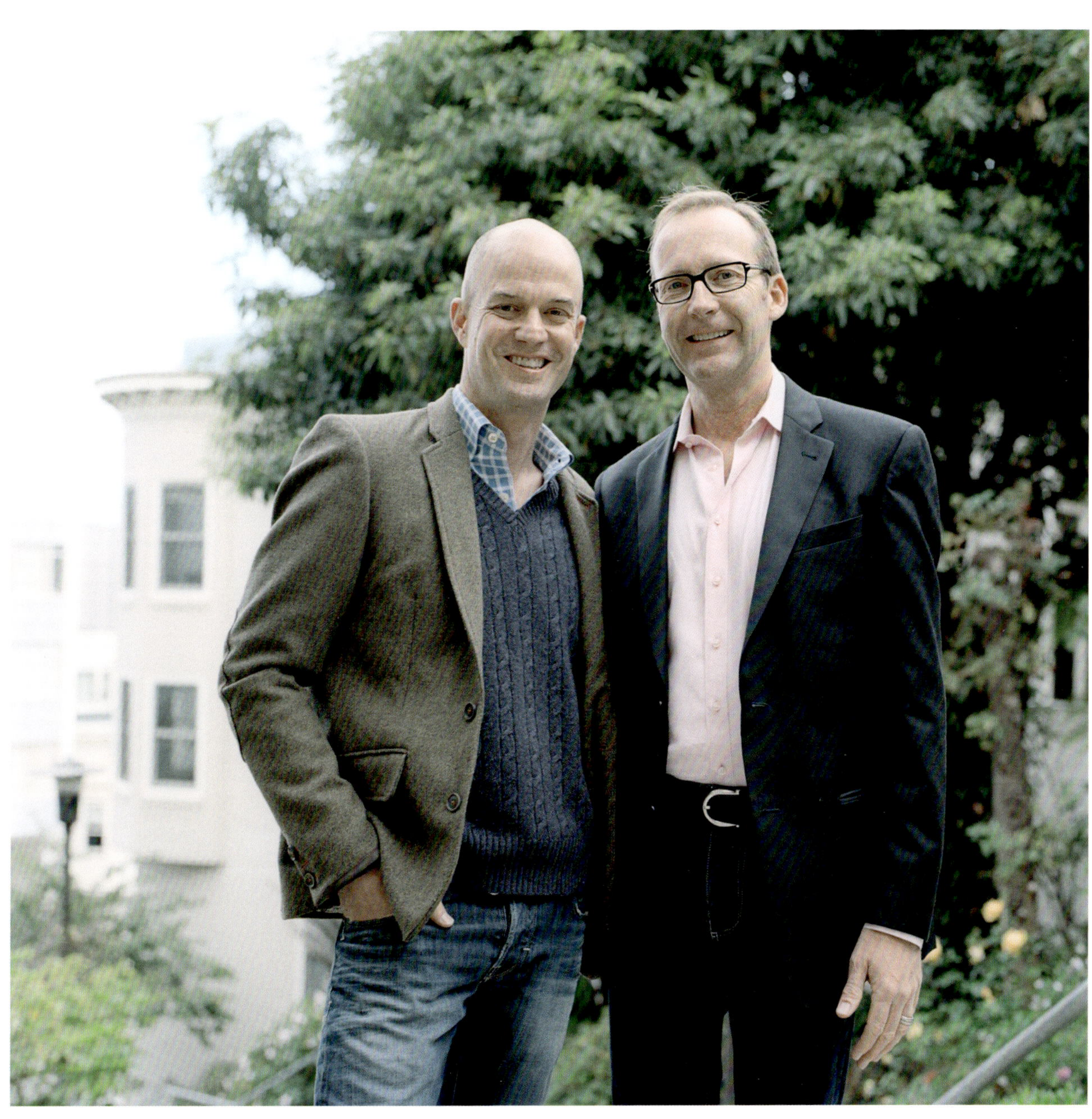

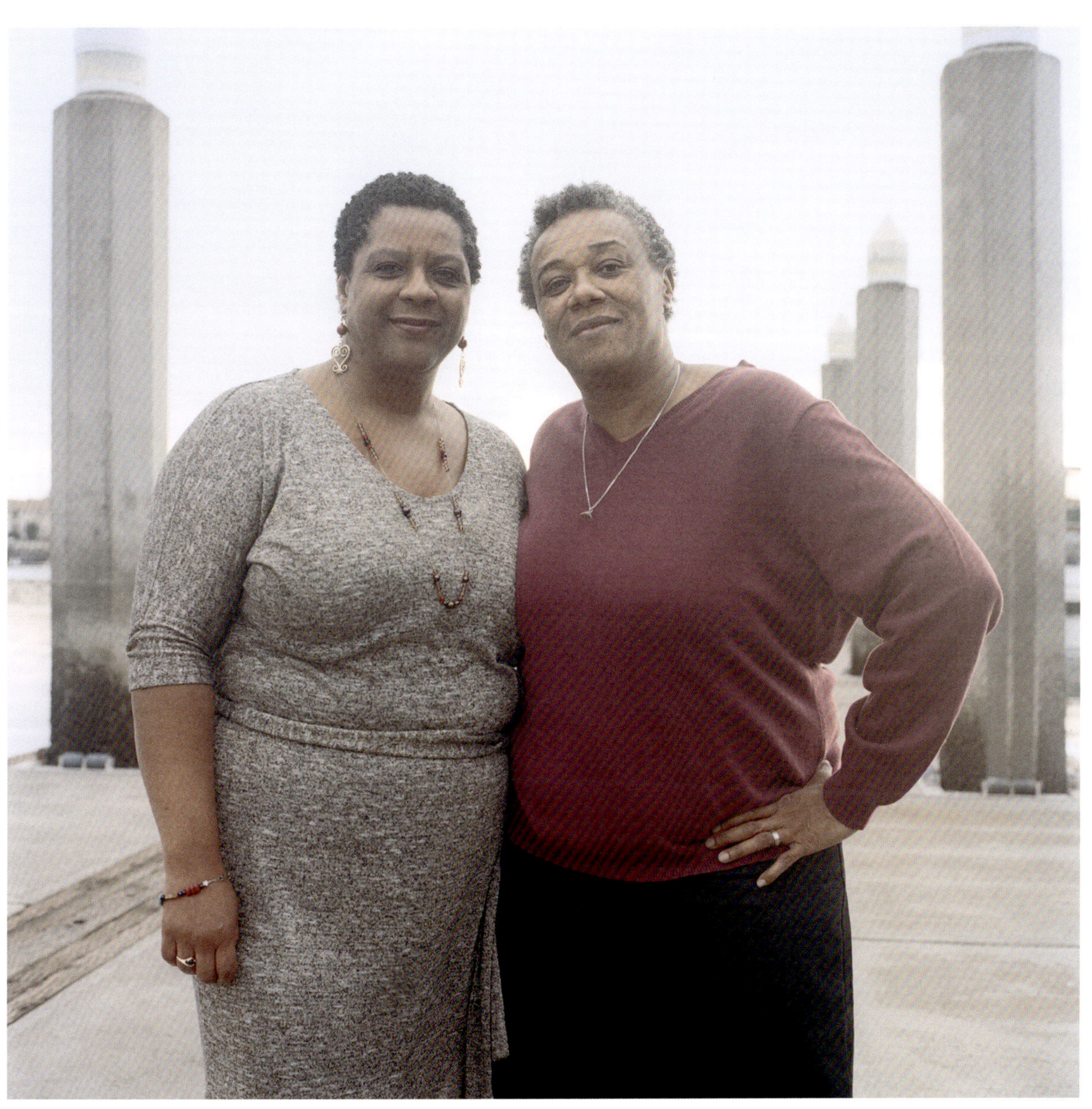

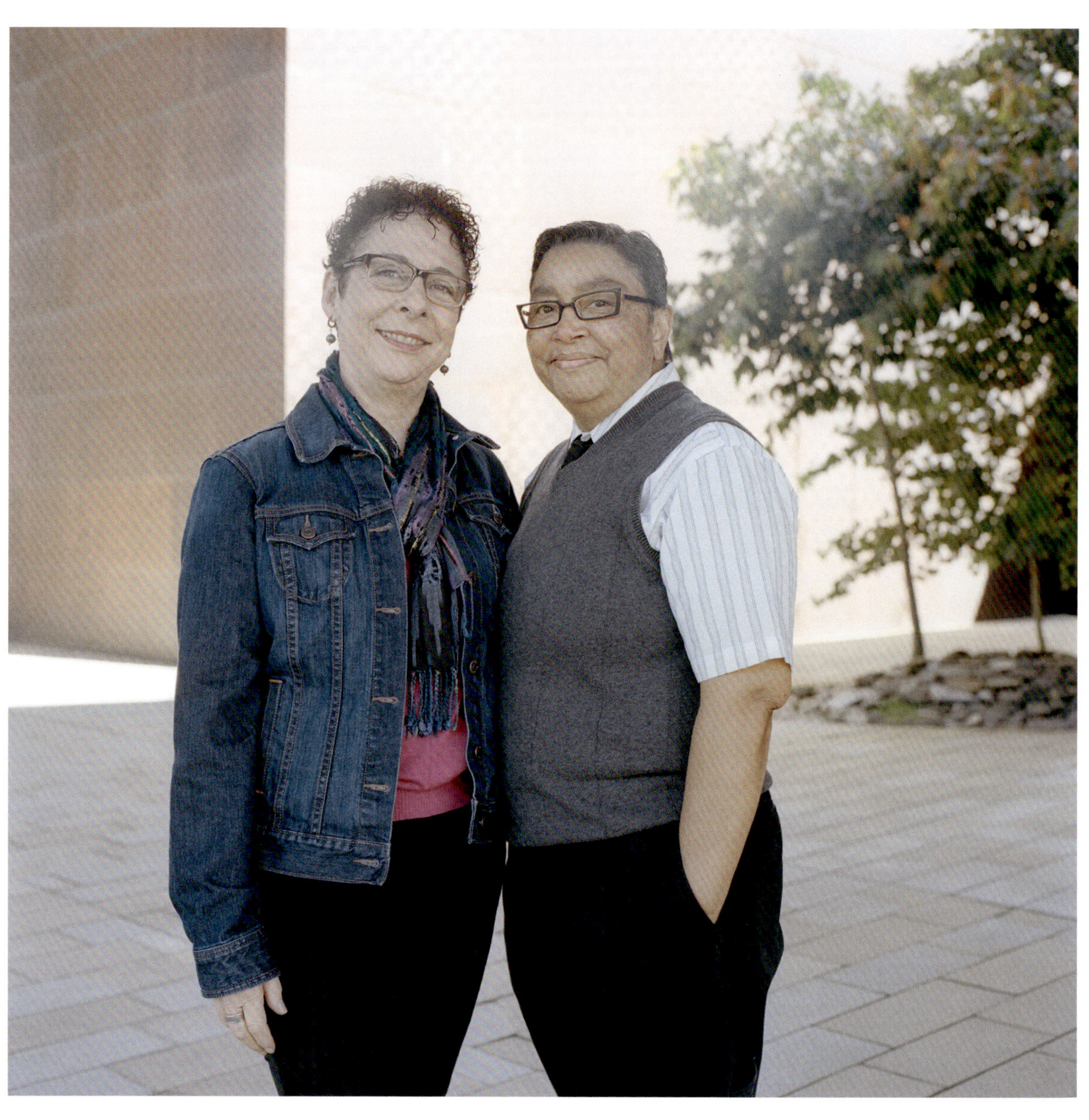

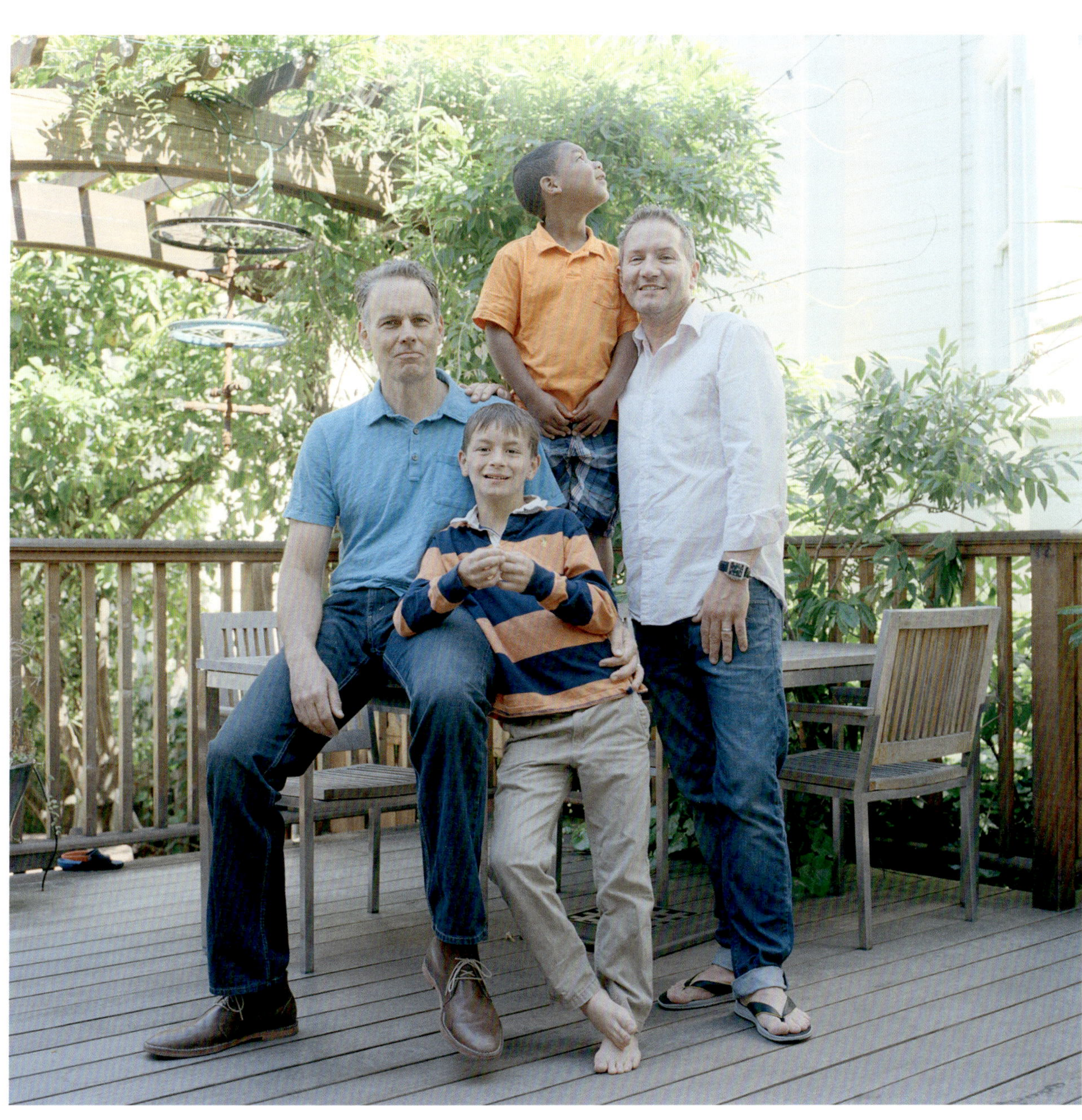

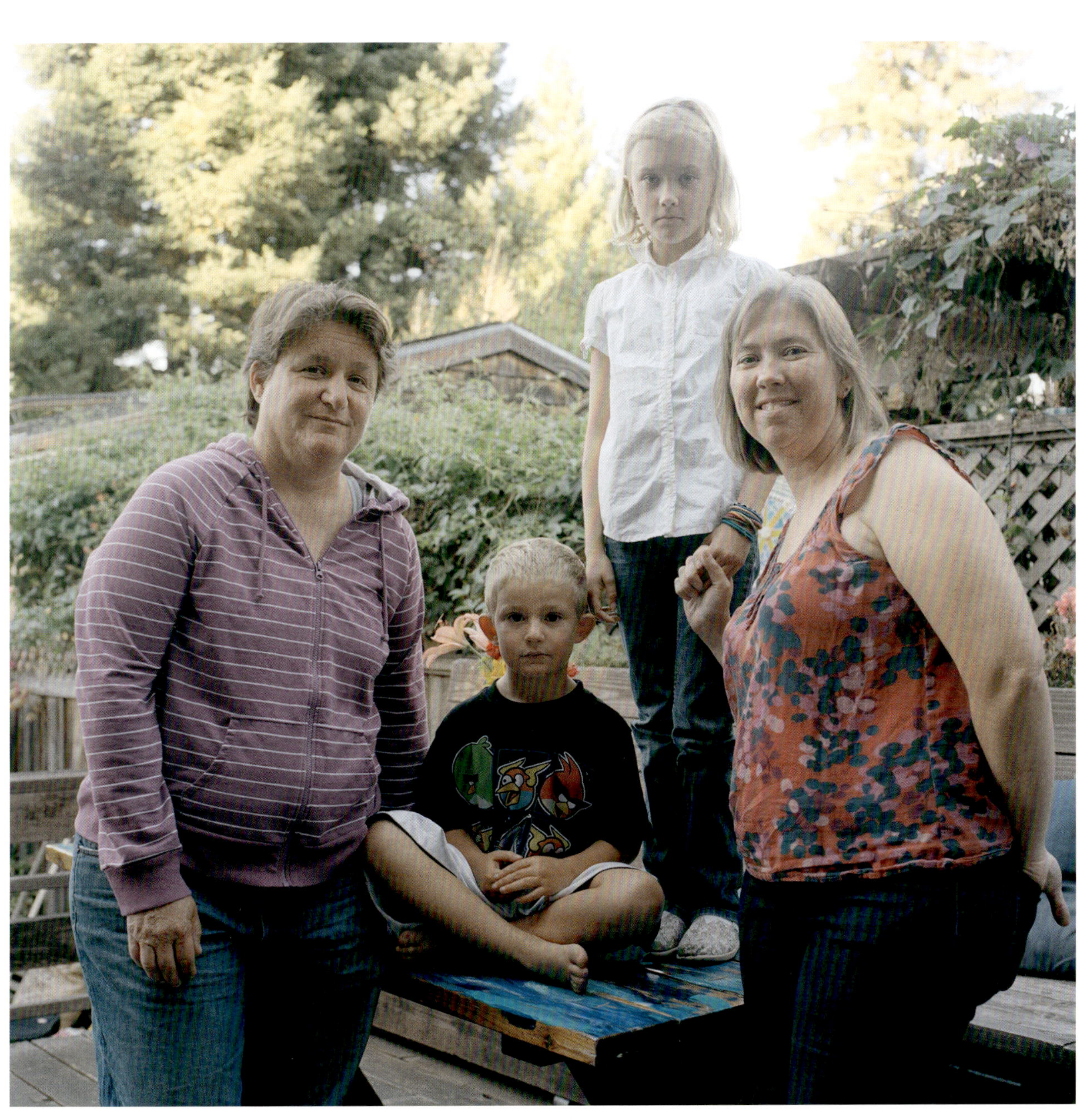

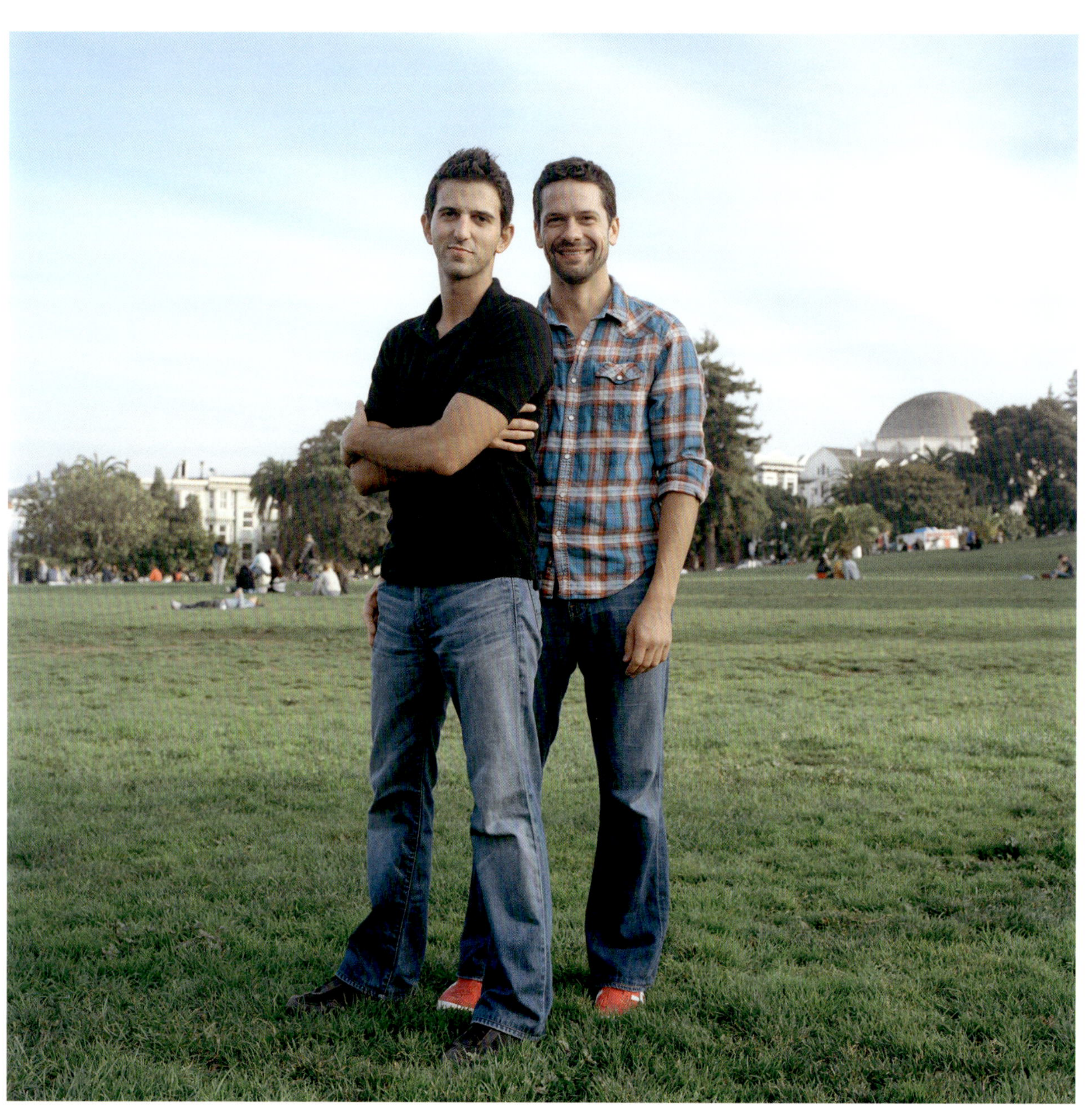

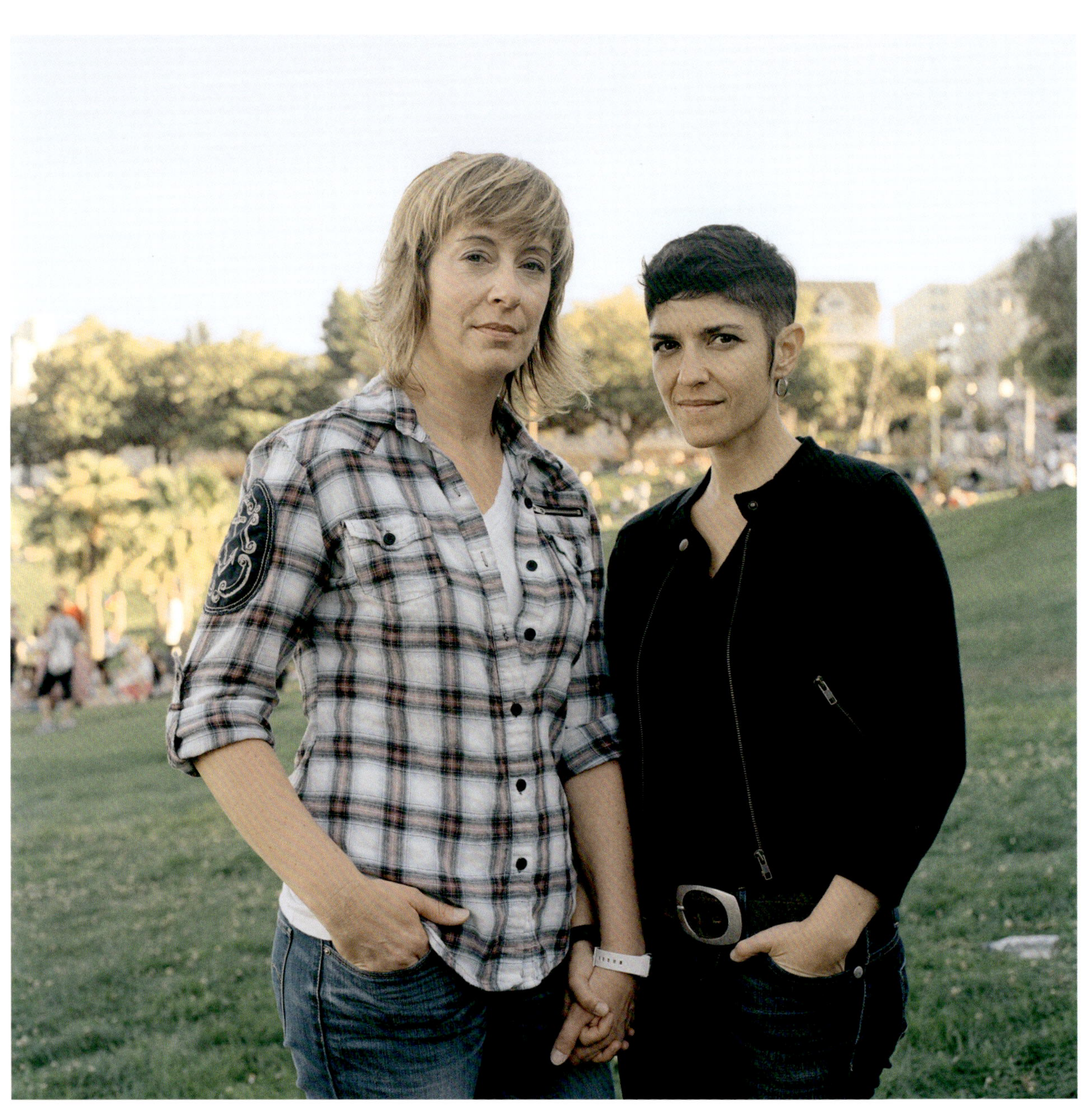

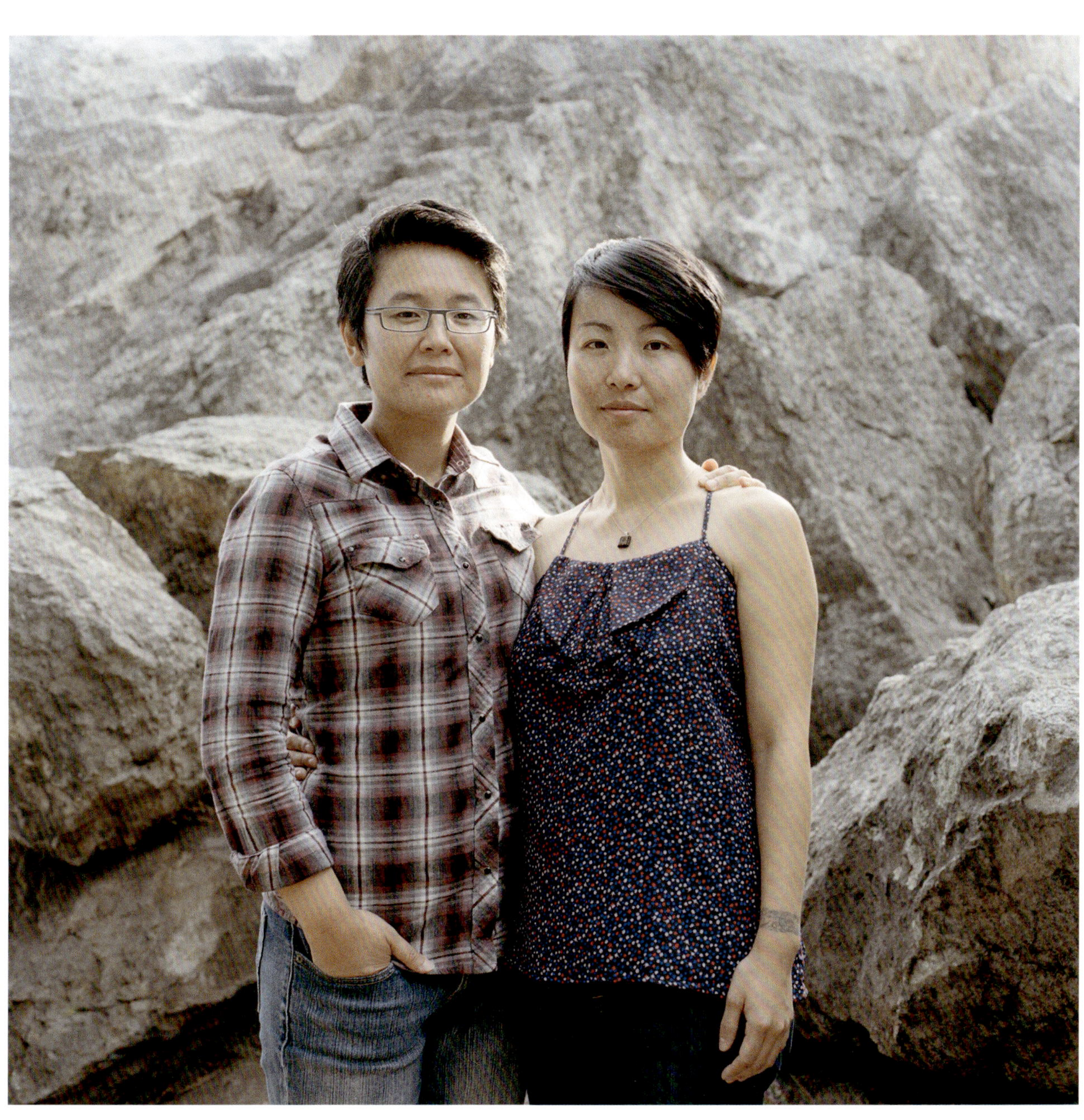

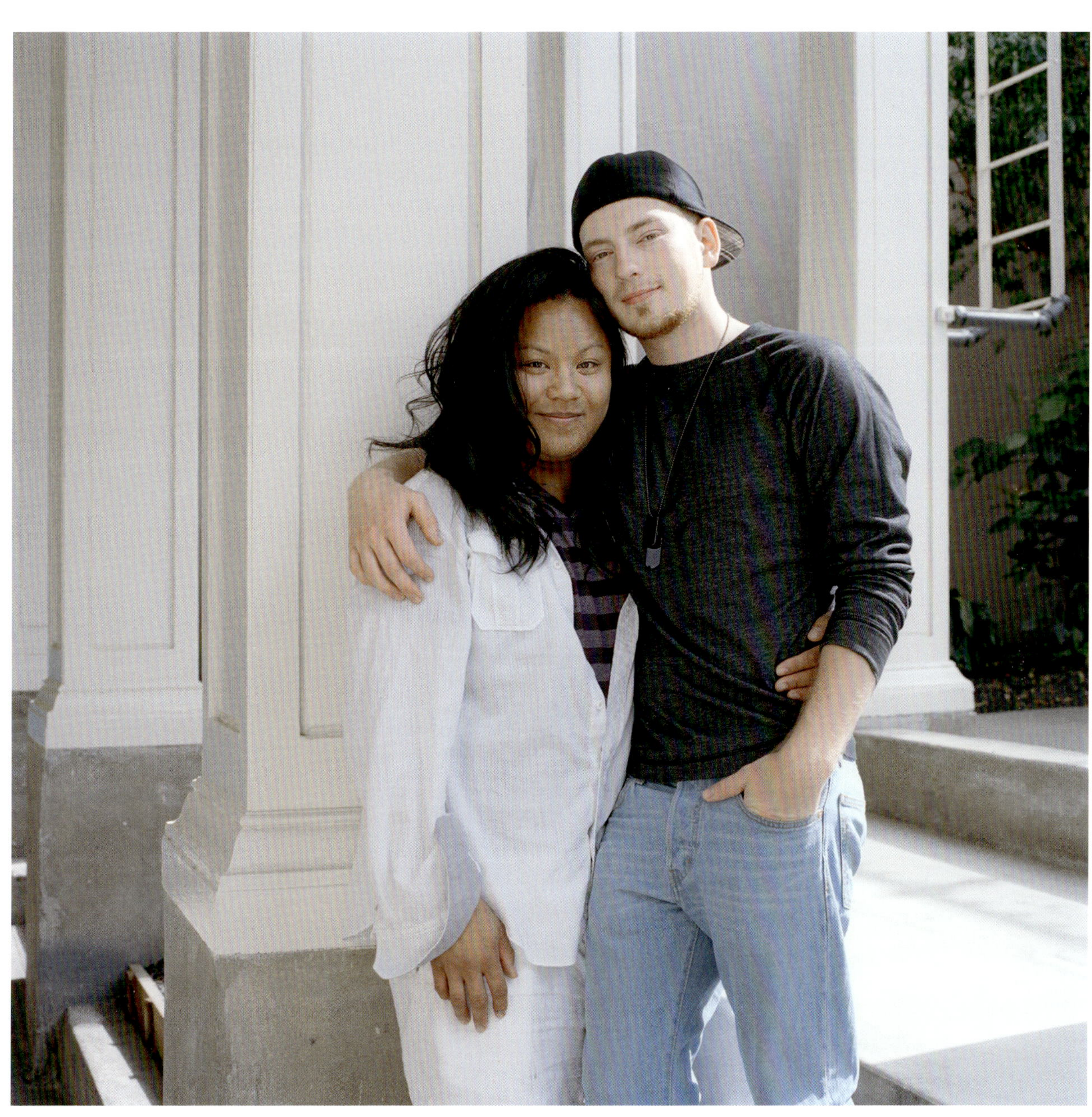

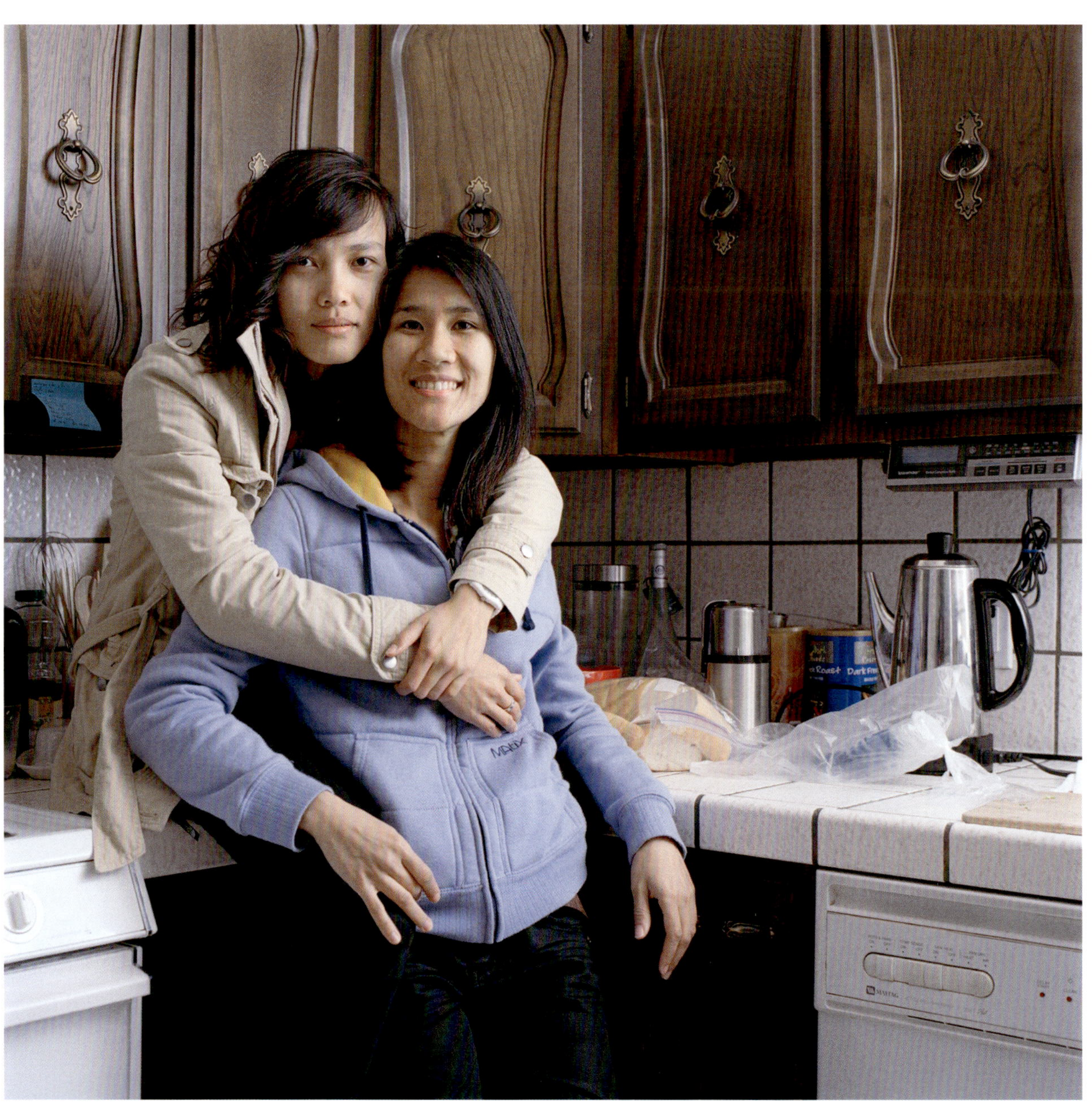

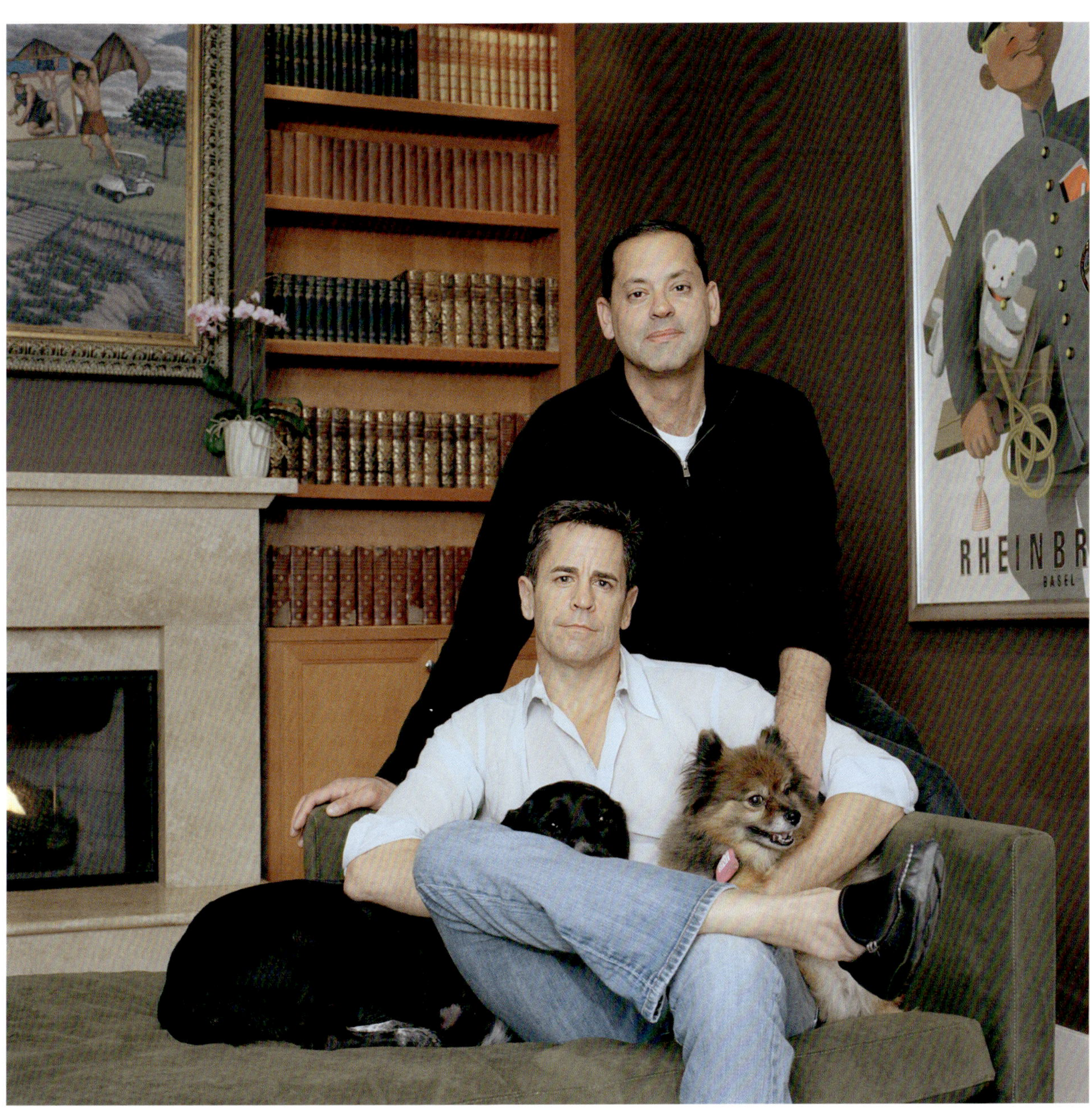
RHEINBR
BASEL

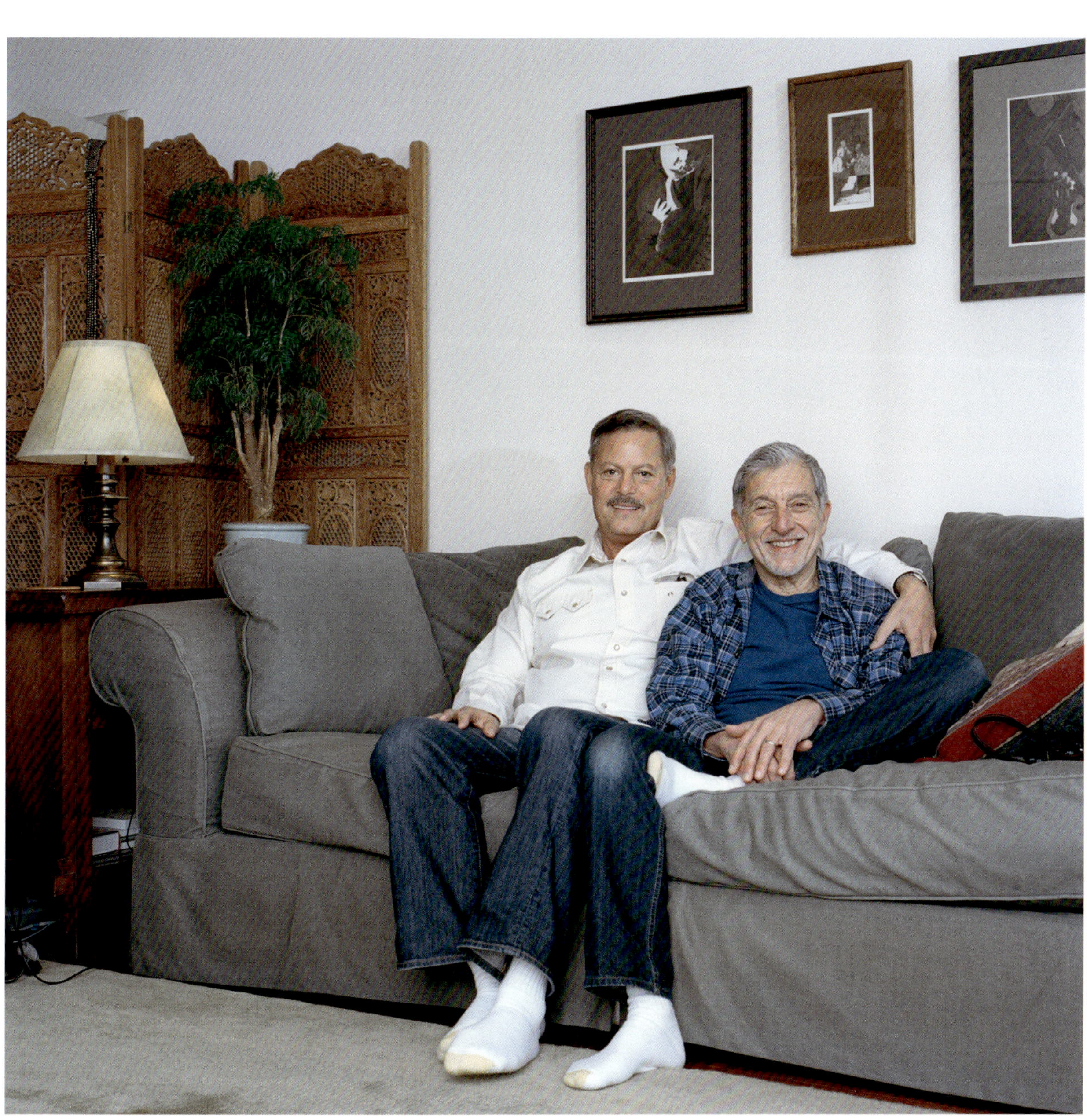

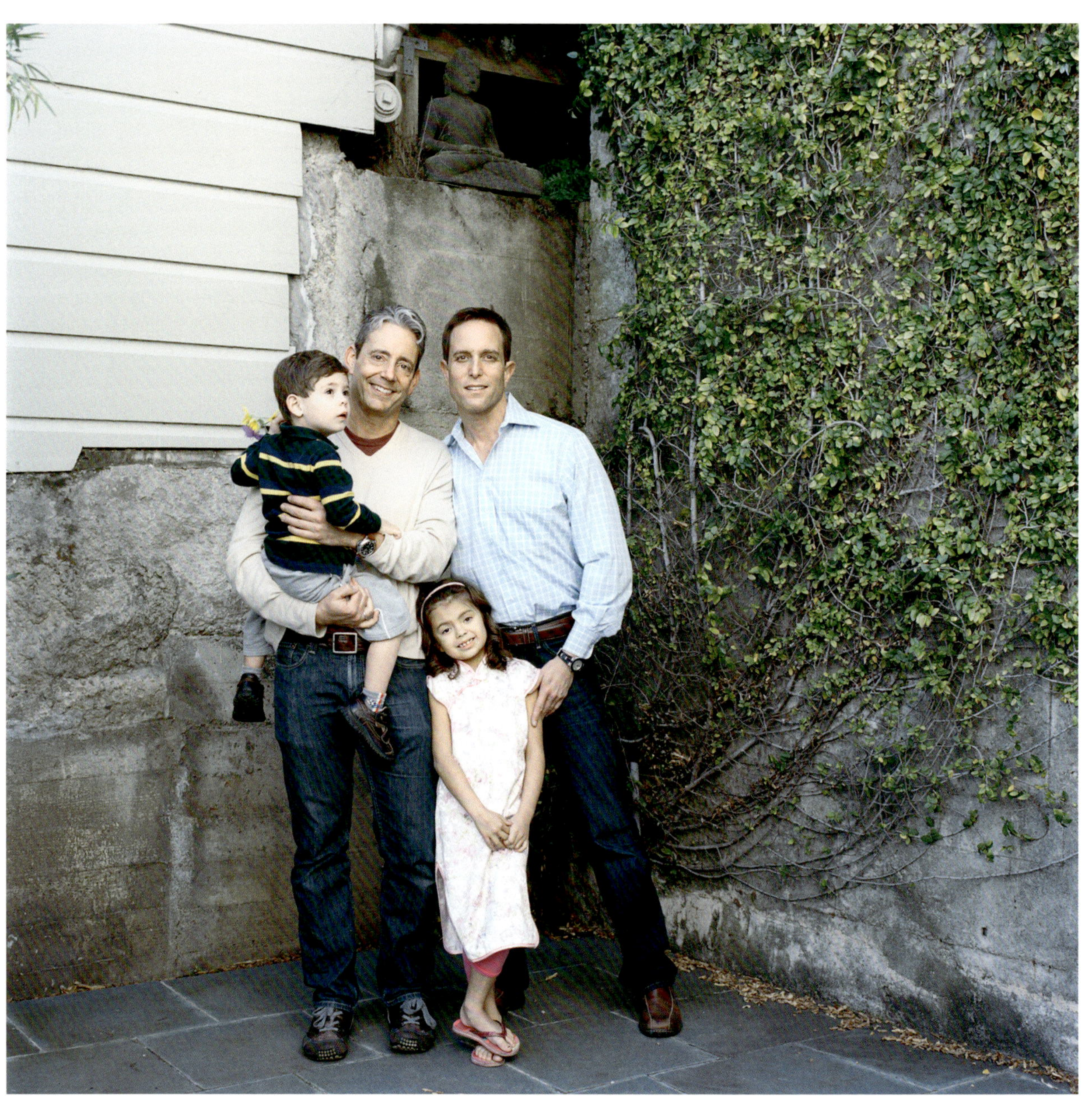

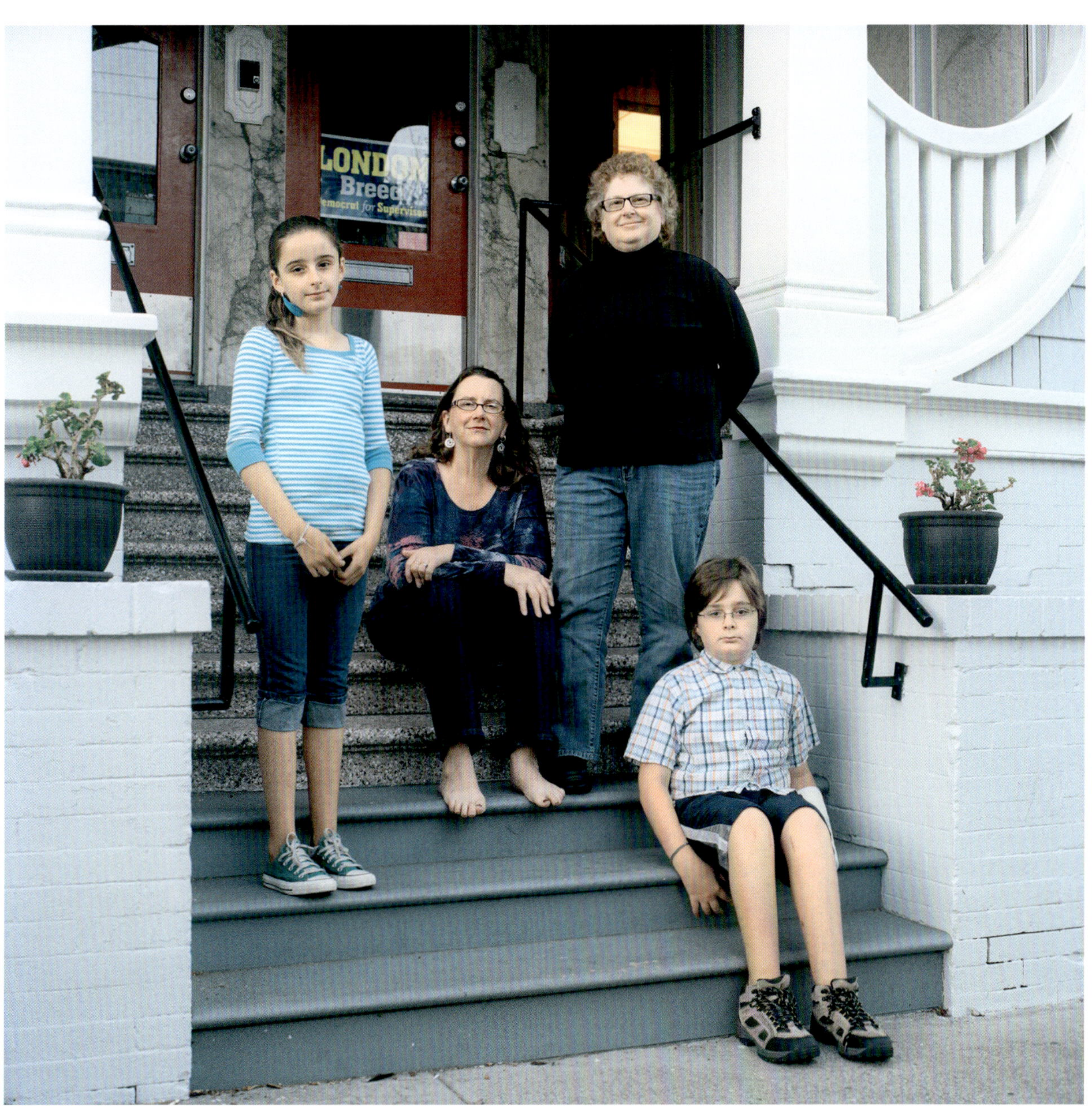
for

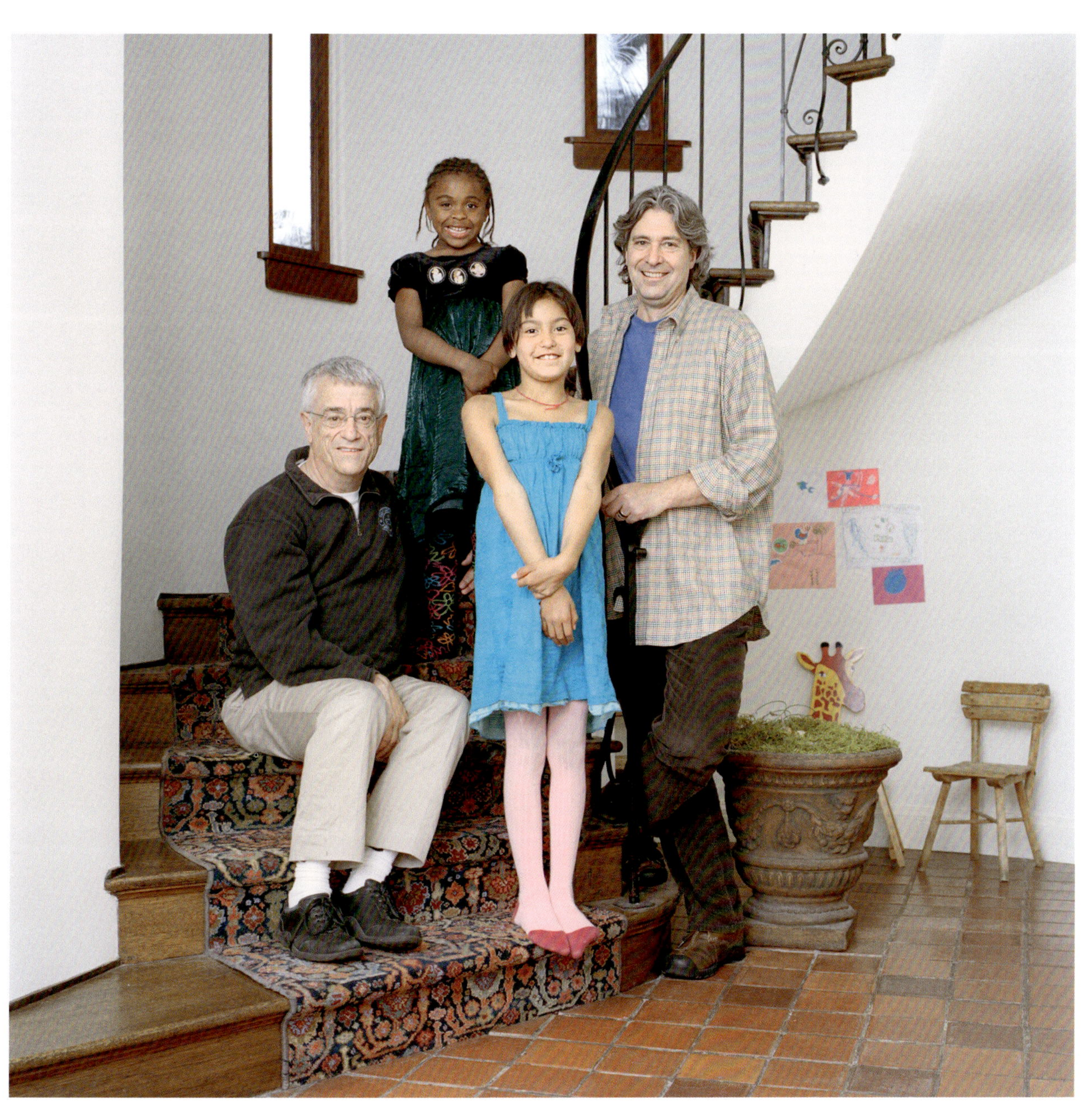

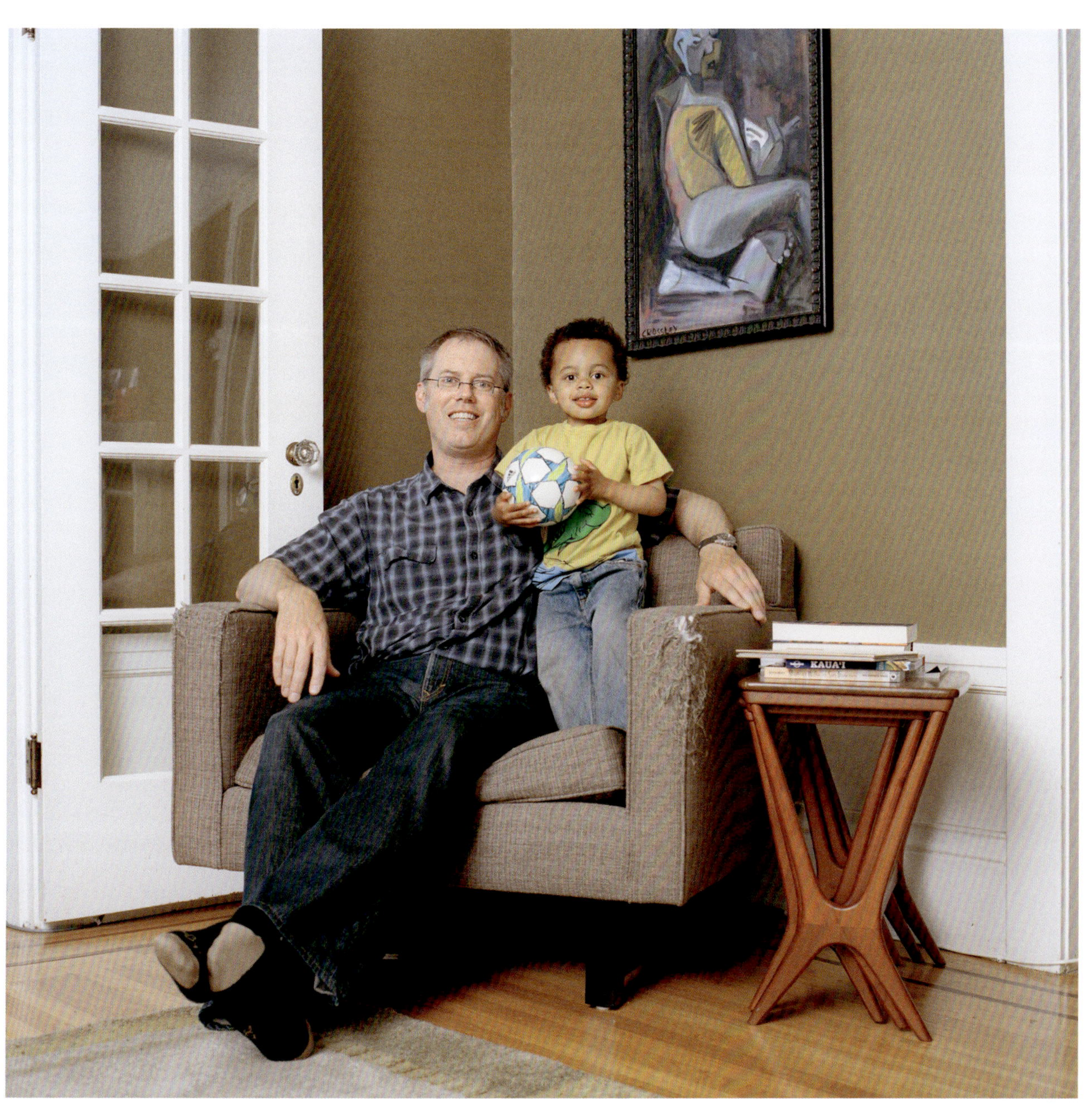
KAUA'I

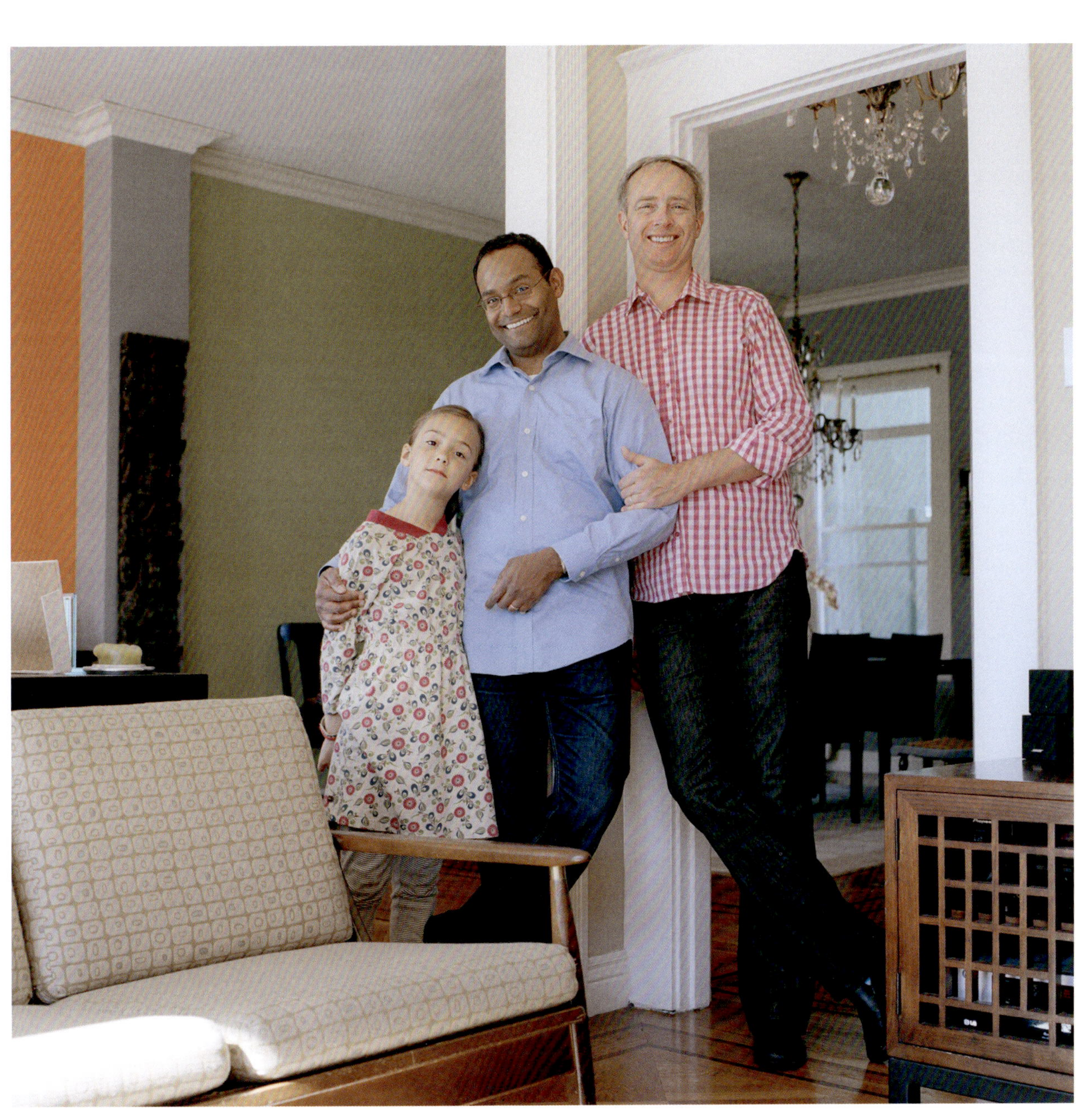

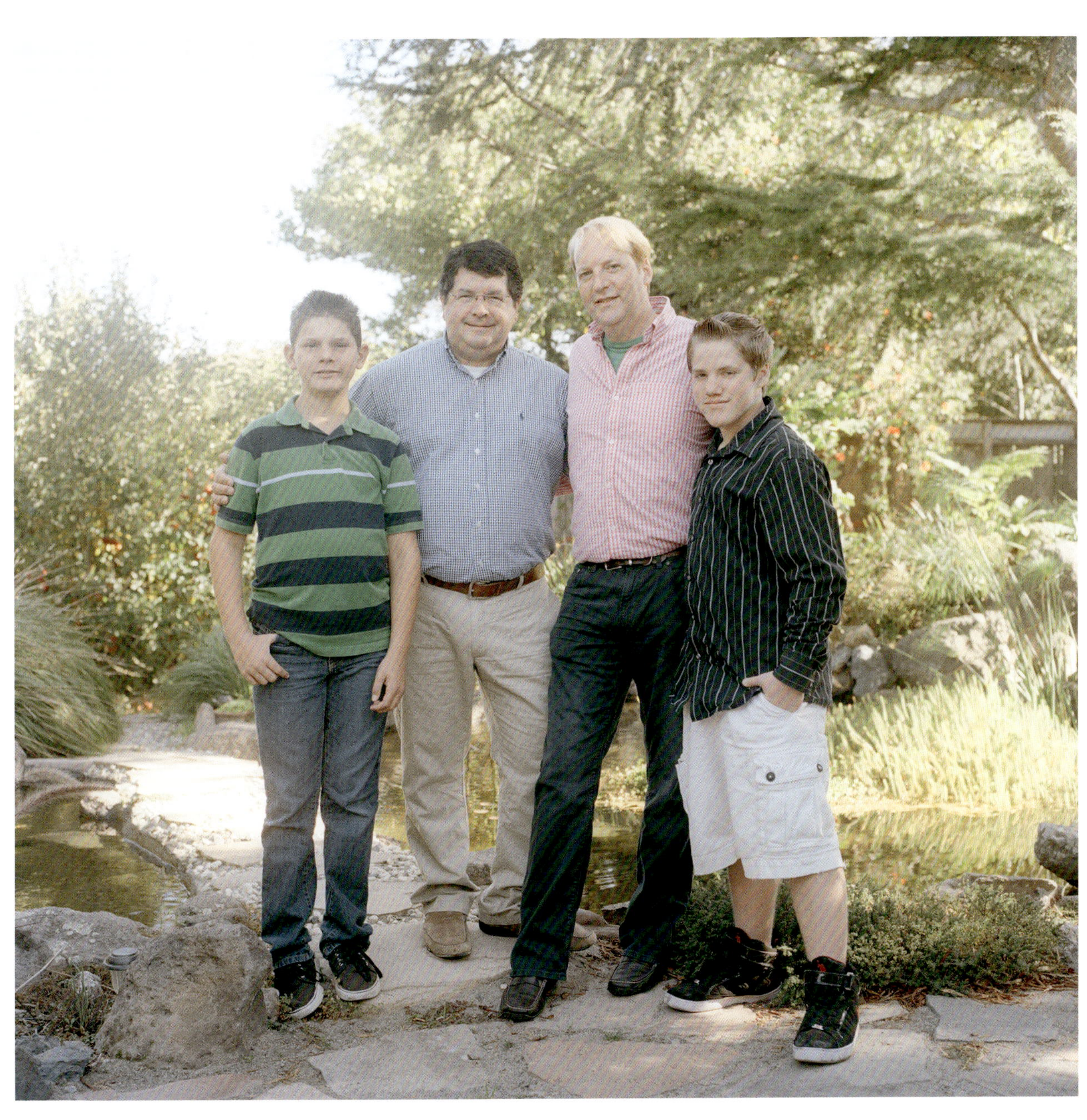

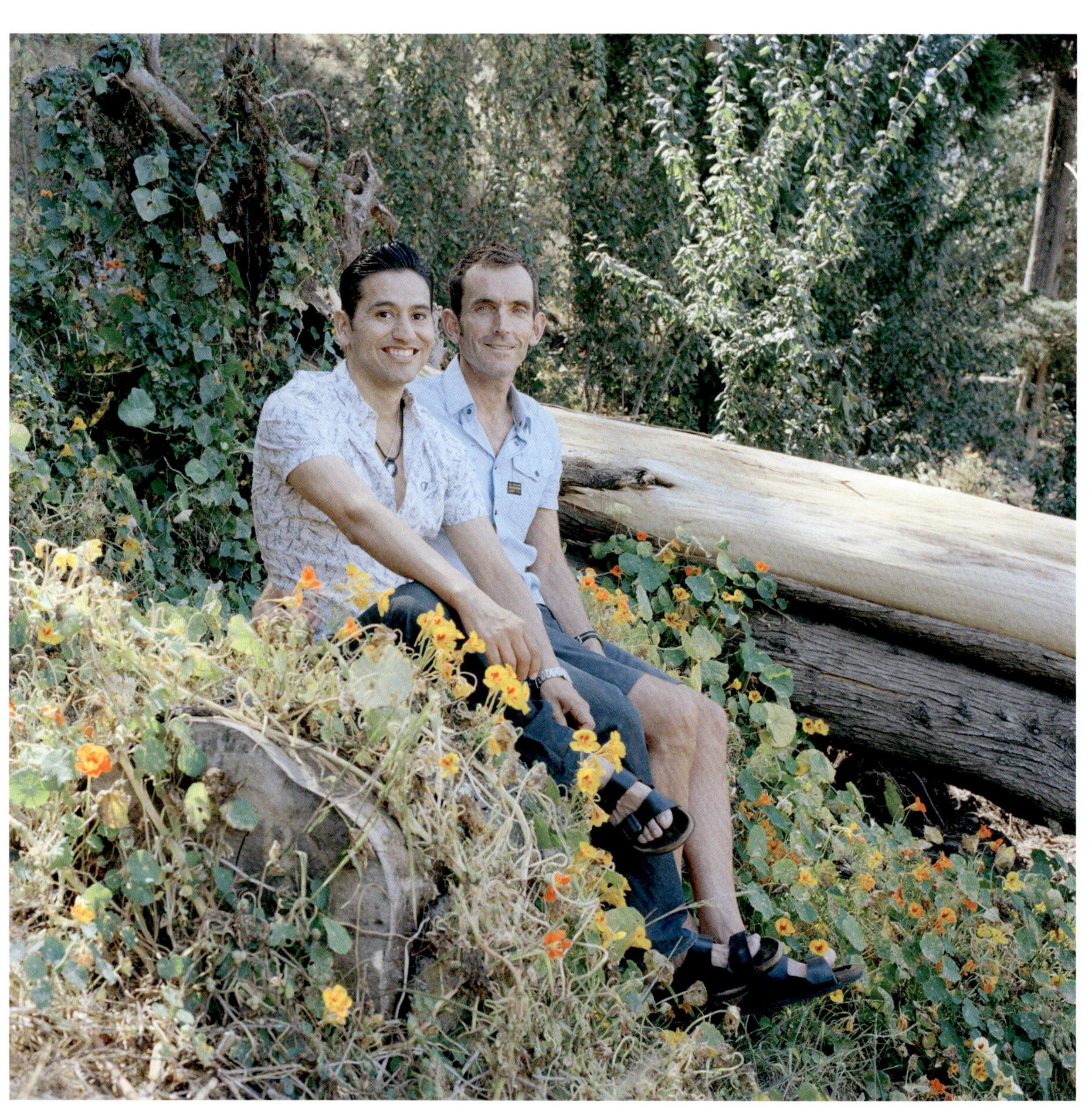

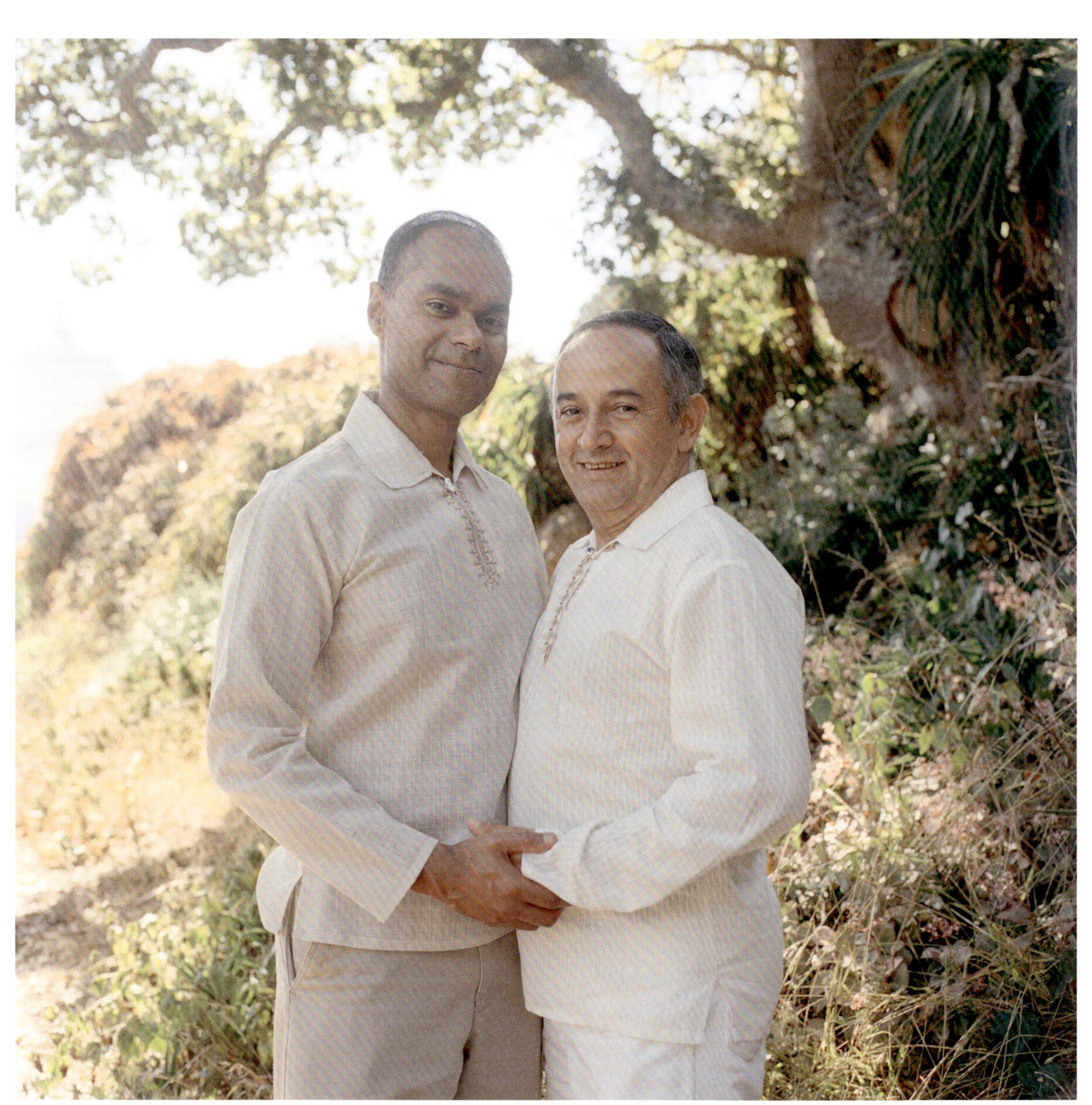

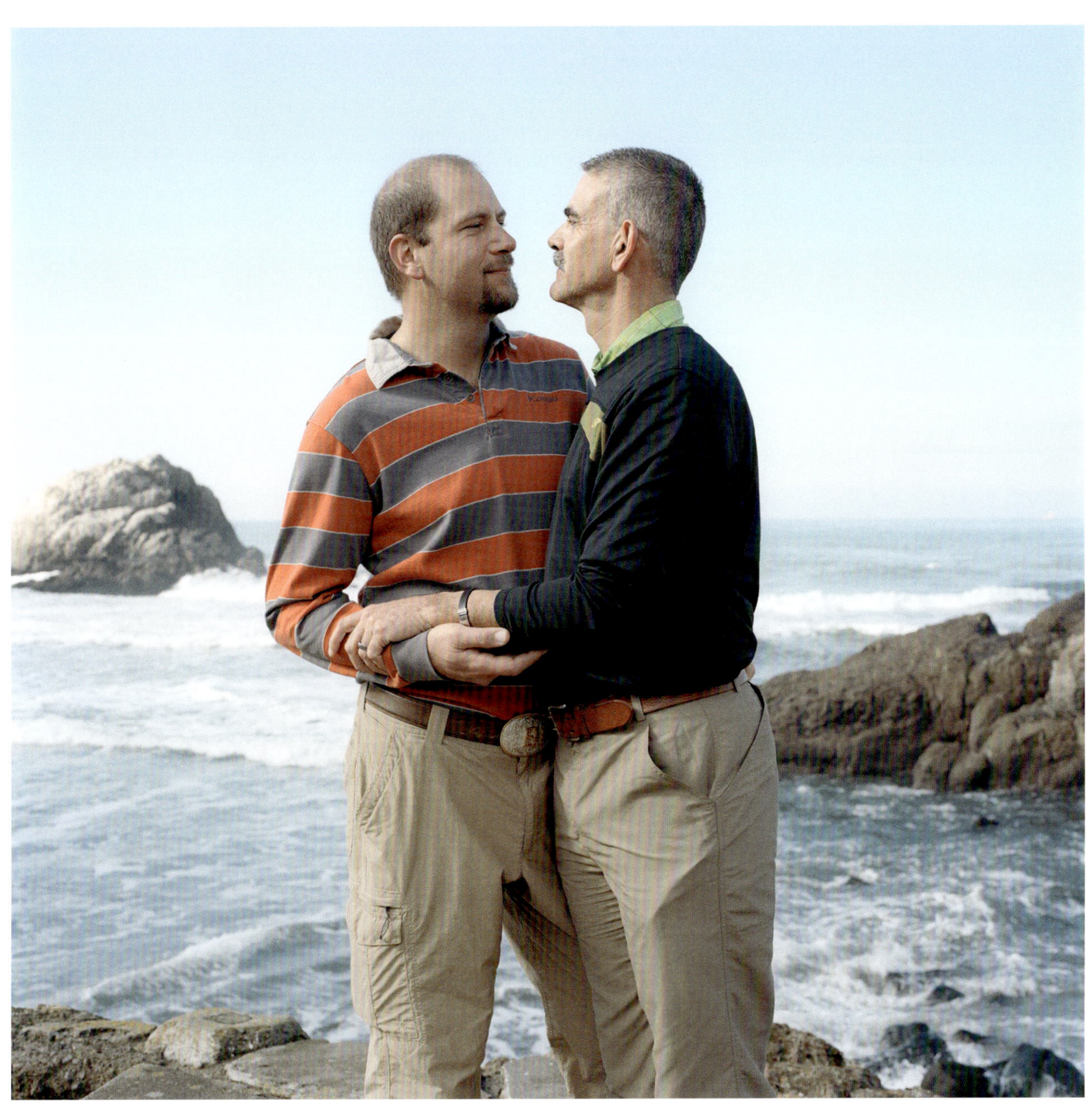

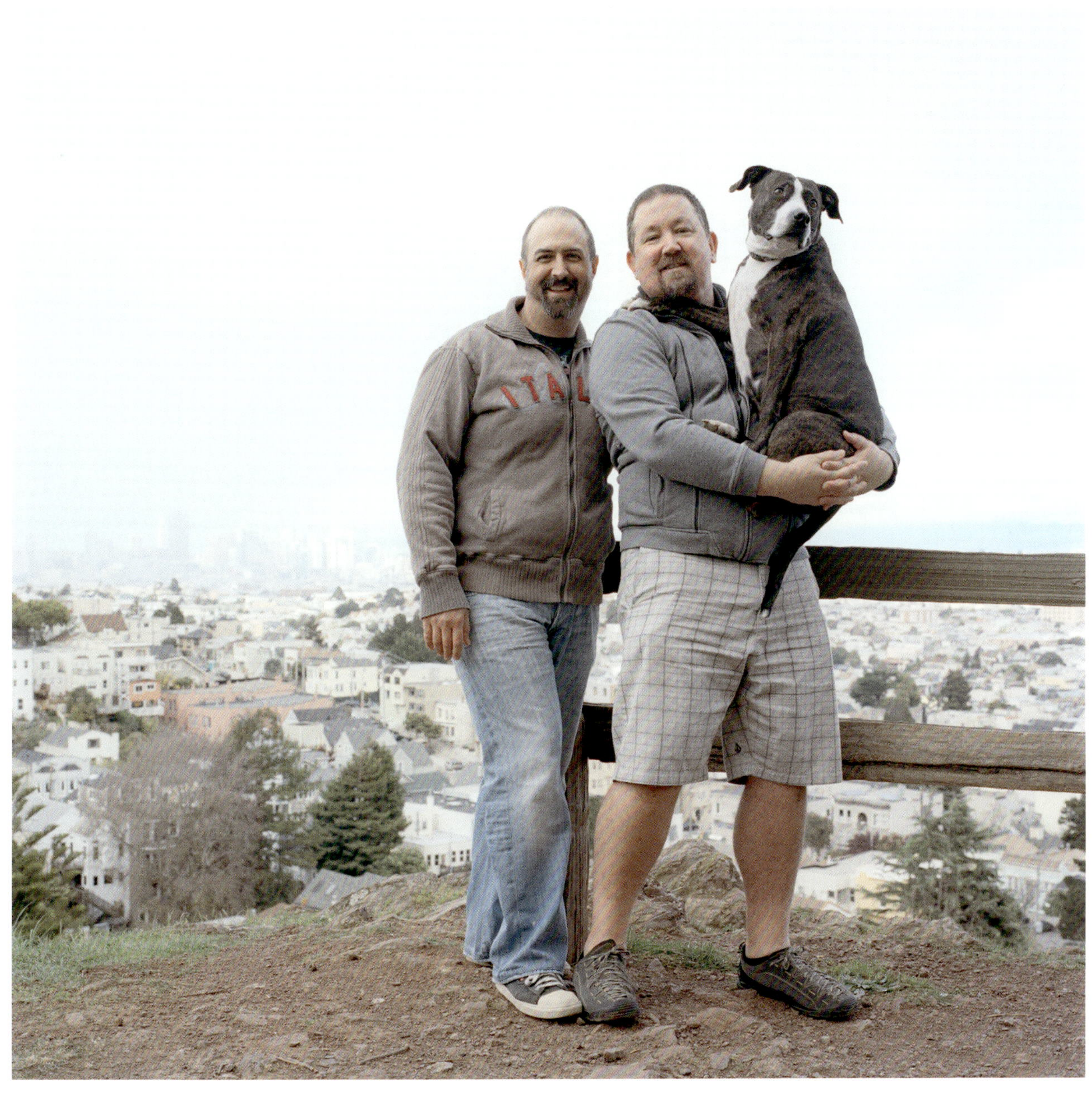

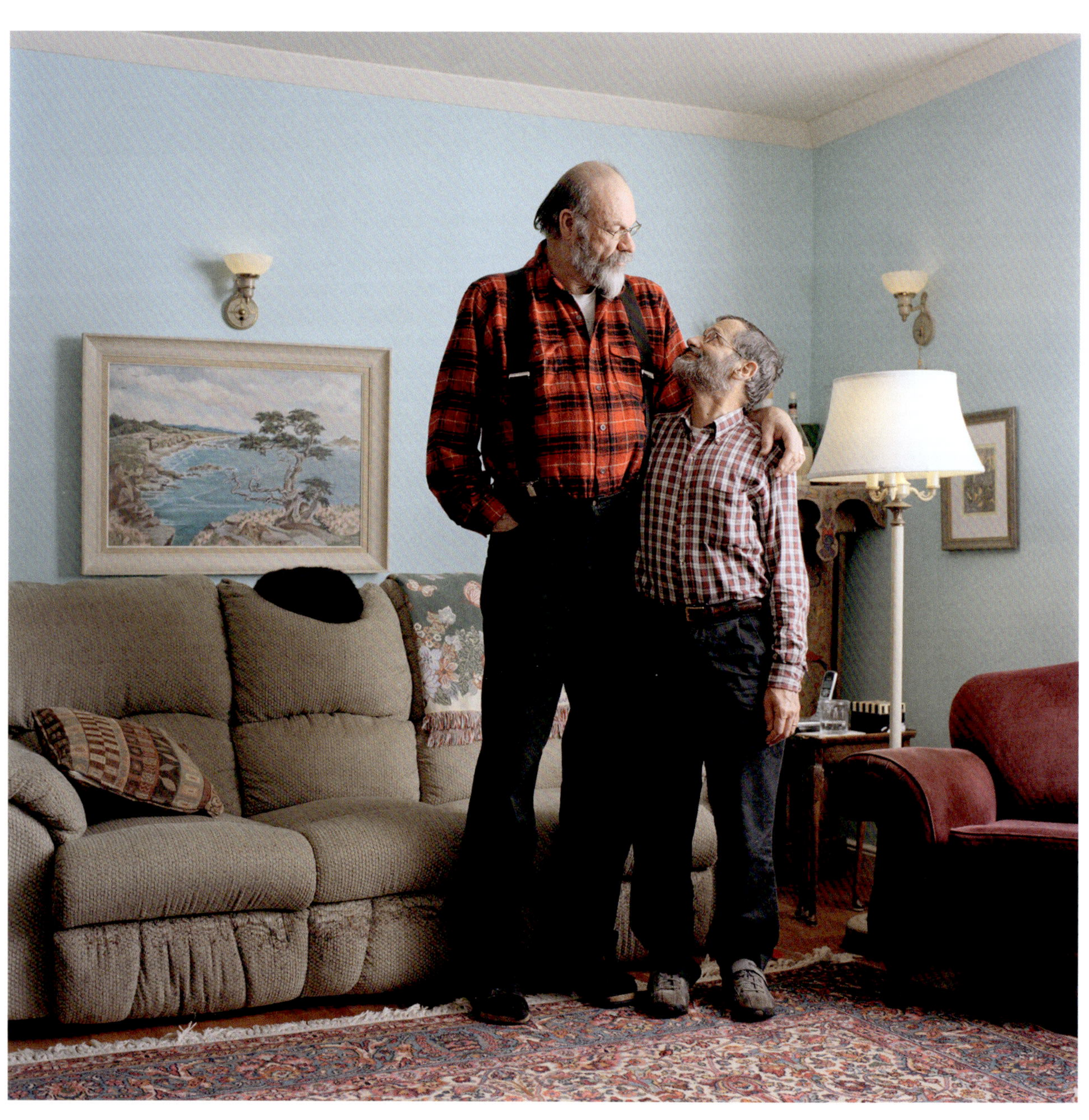

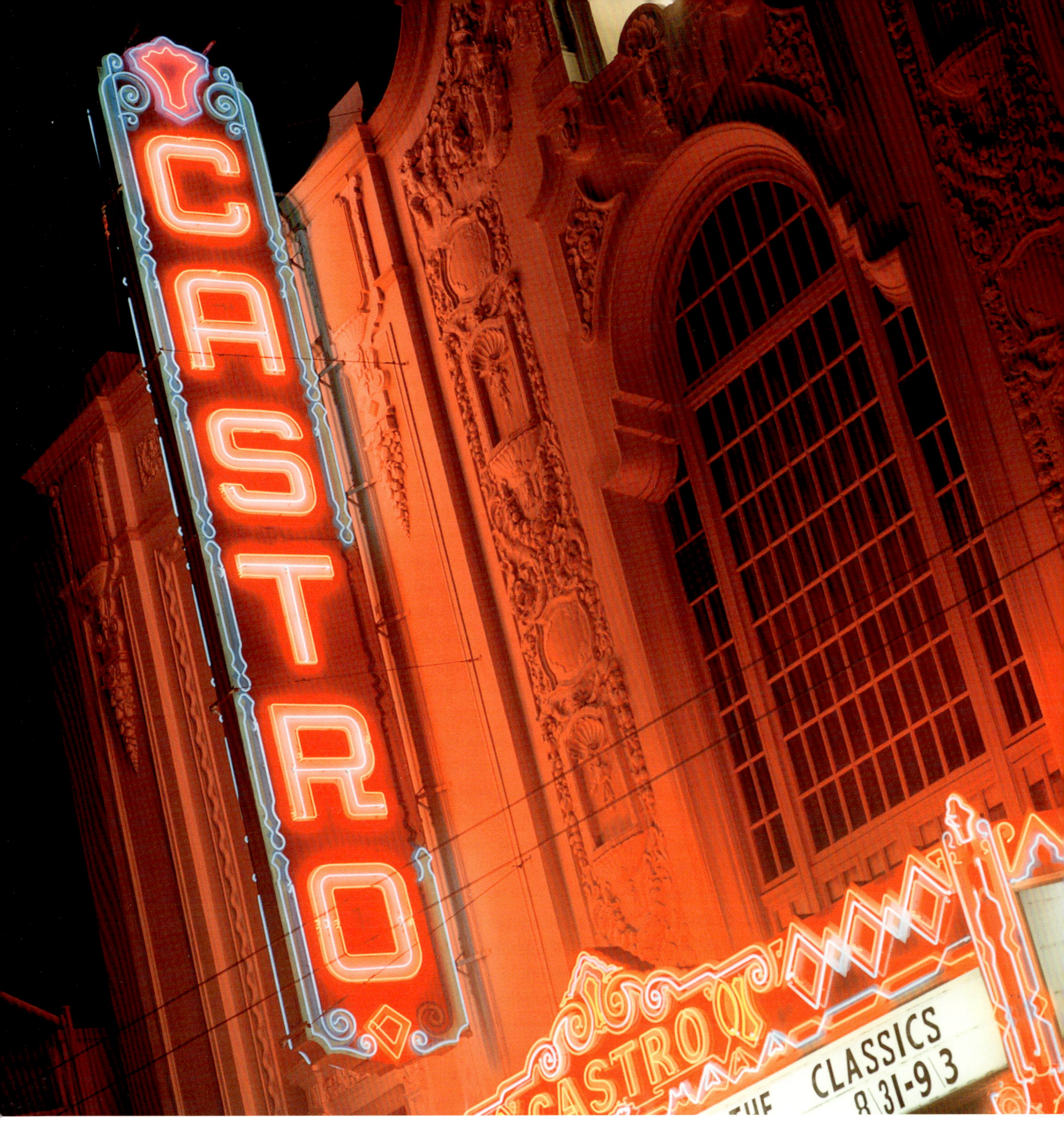
CASTRO
CASTRO
CLASSICS
8 31-9 3

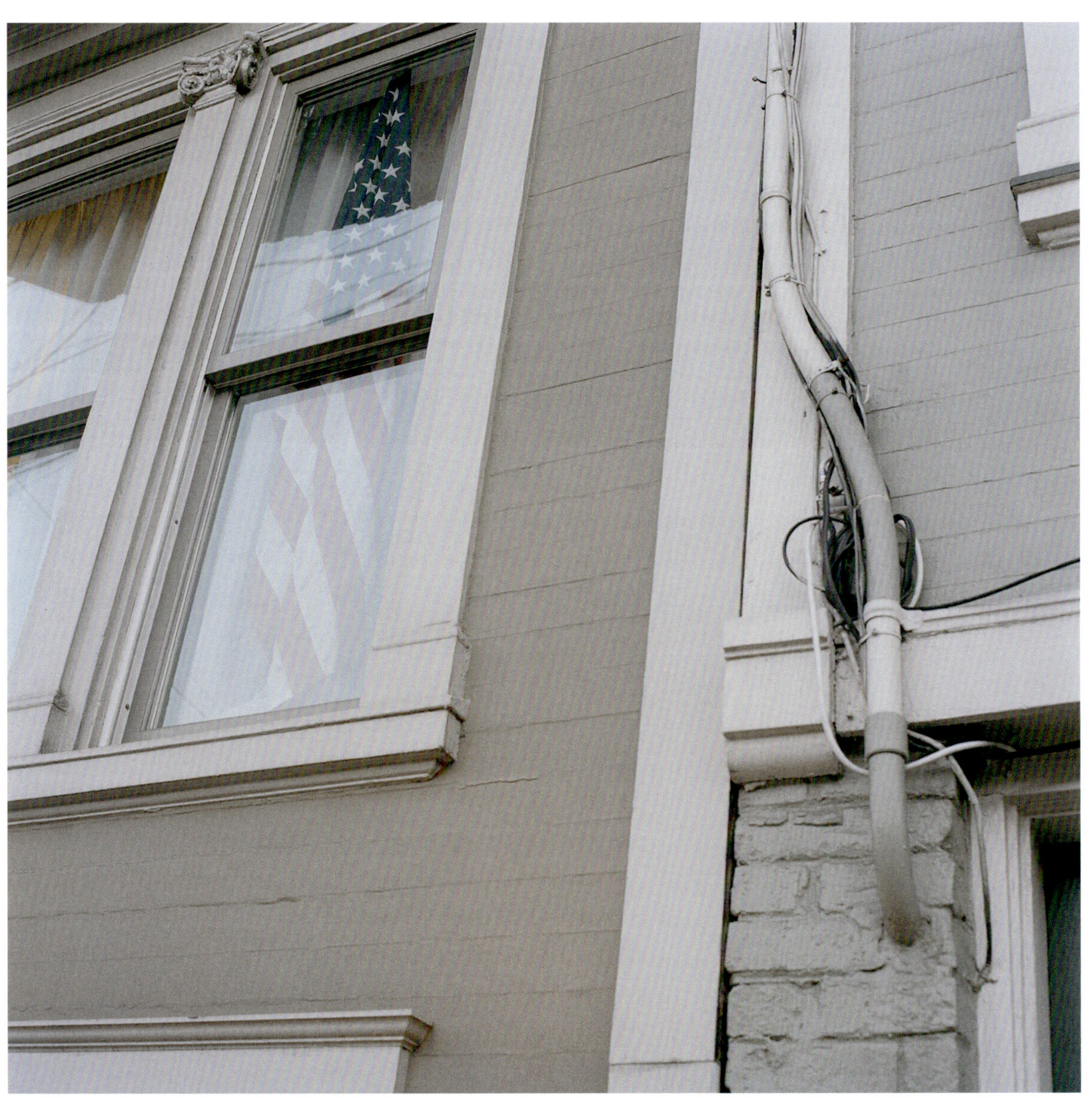

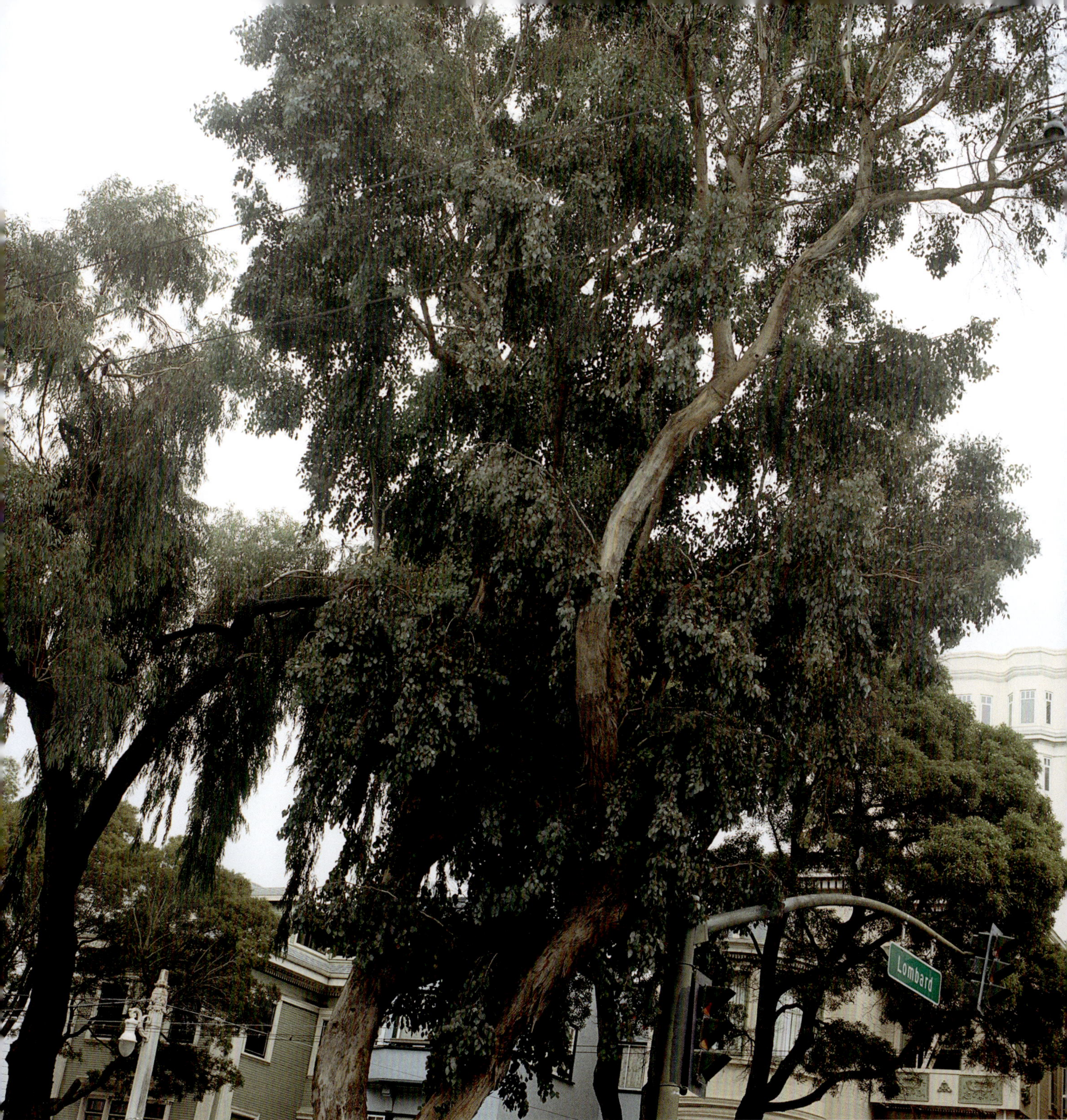
Lombard

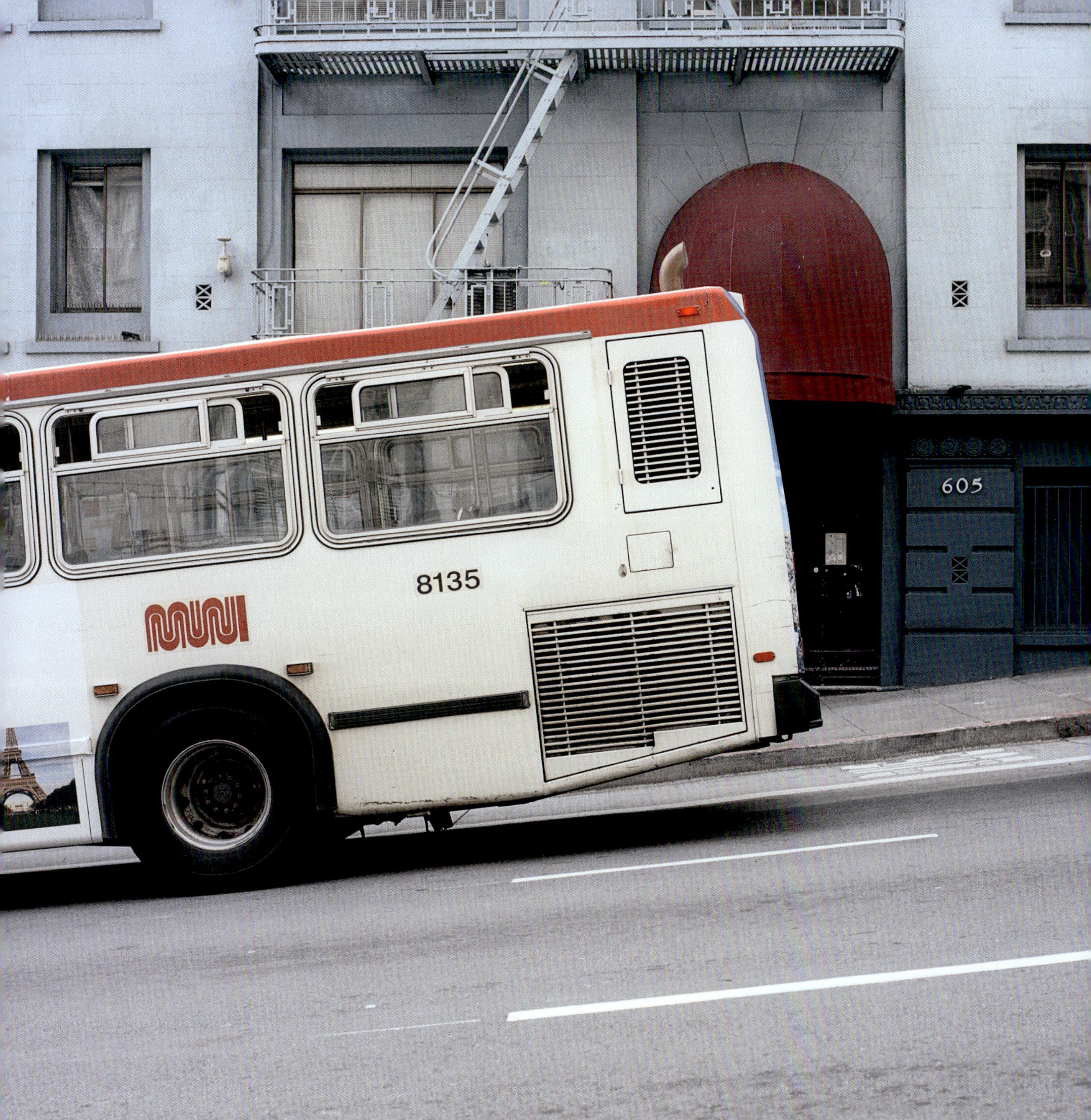
muni
8135
605

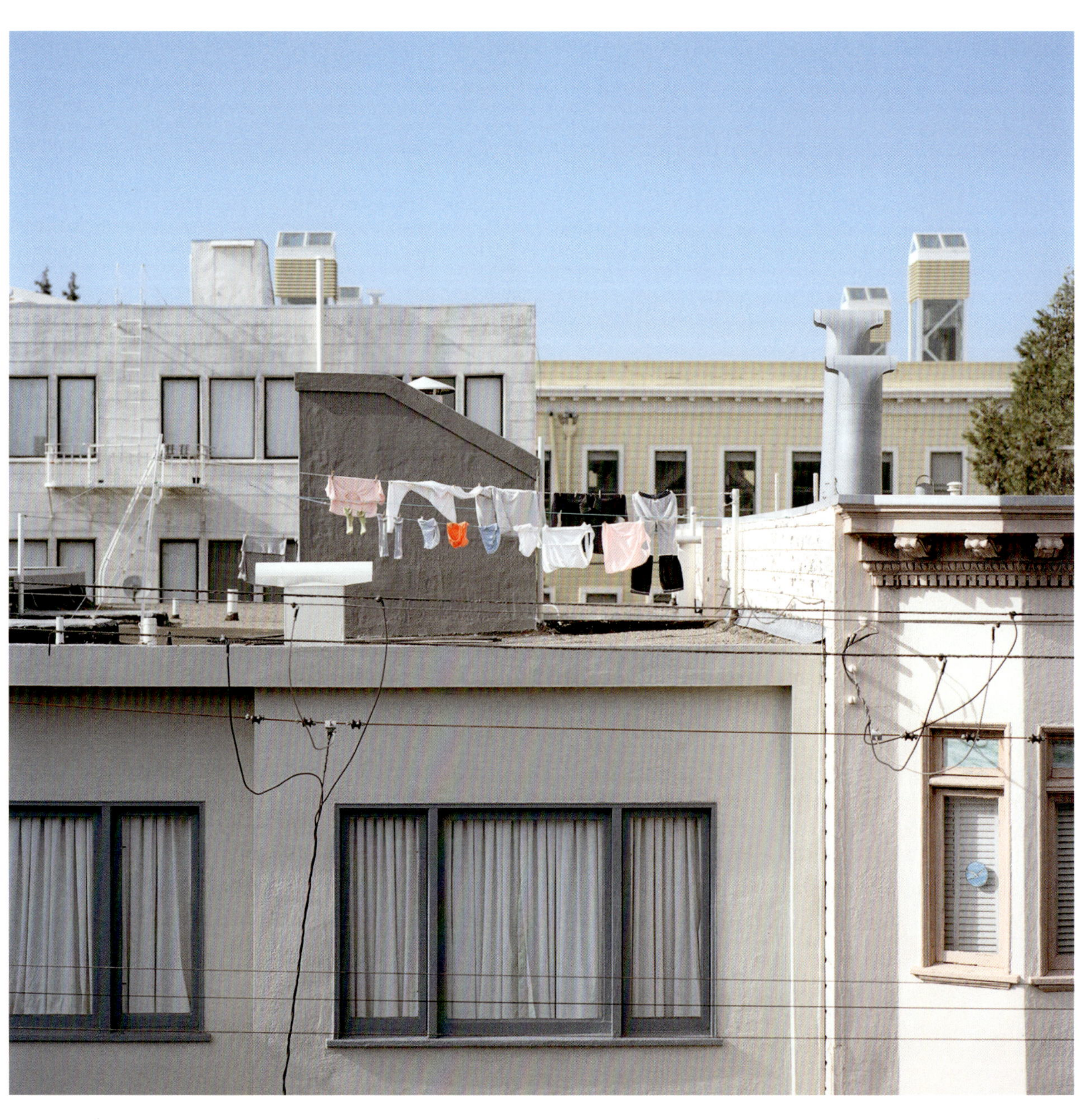

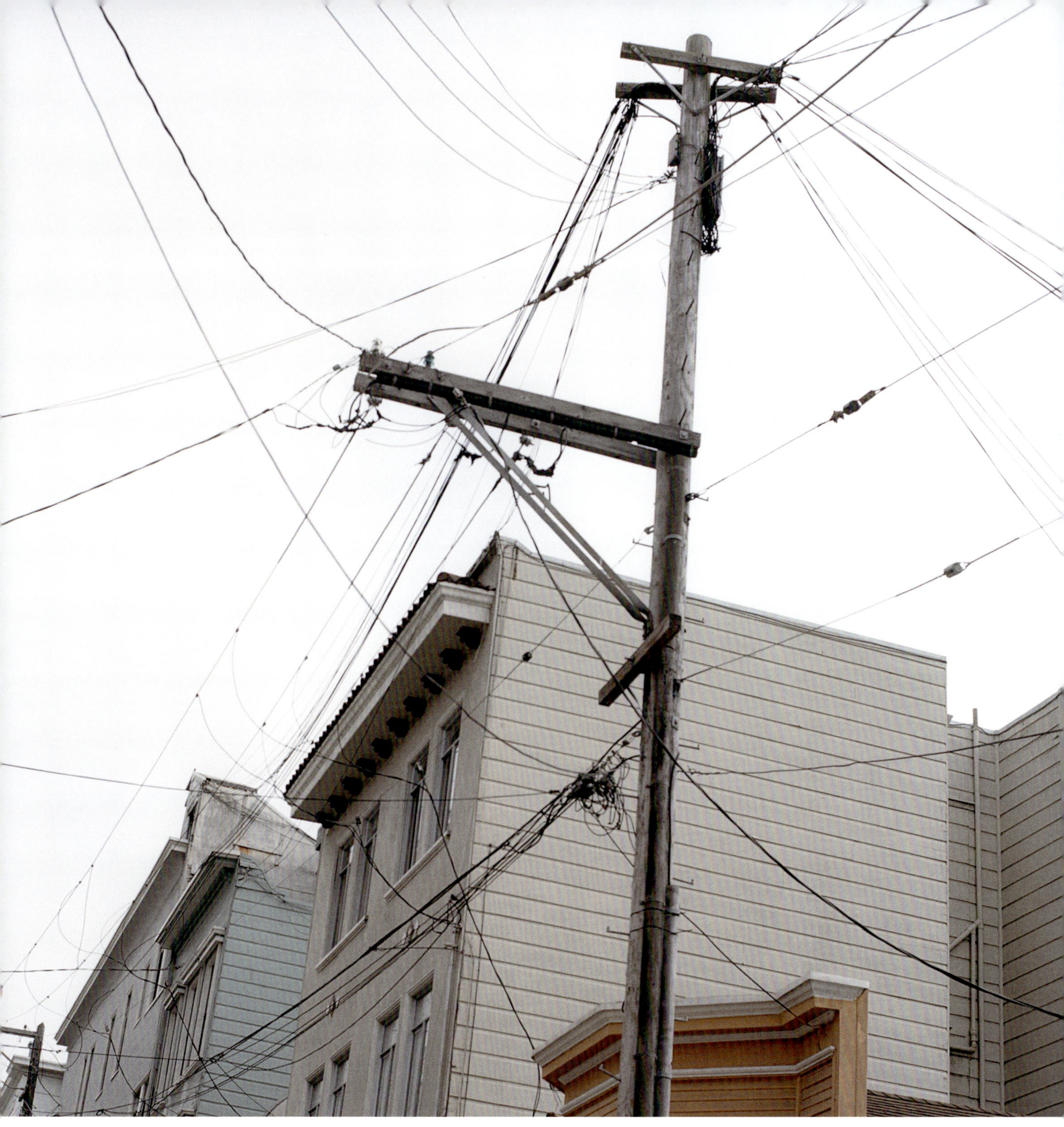

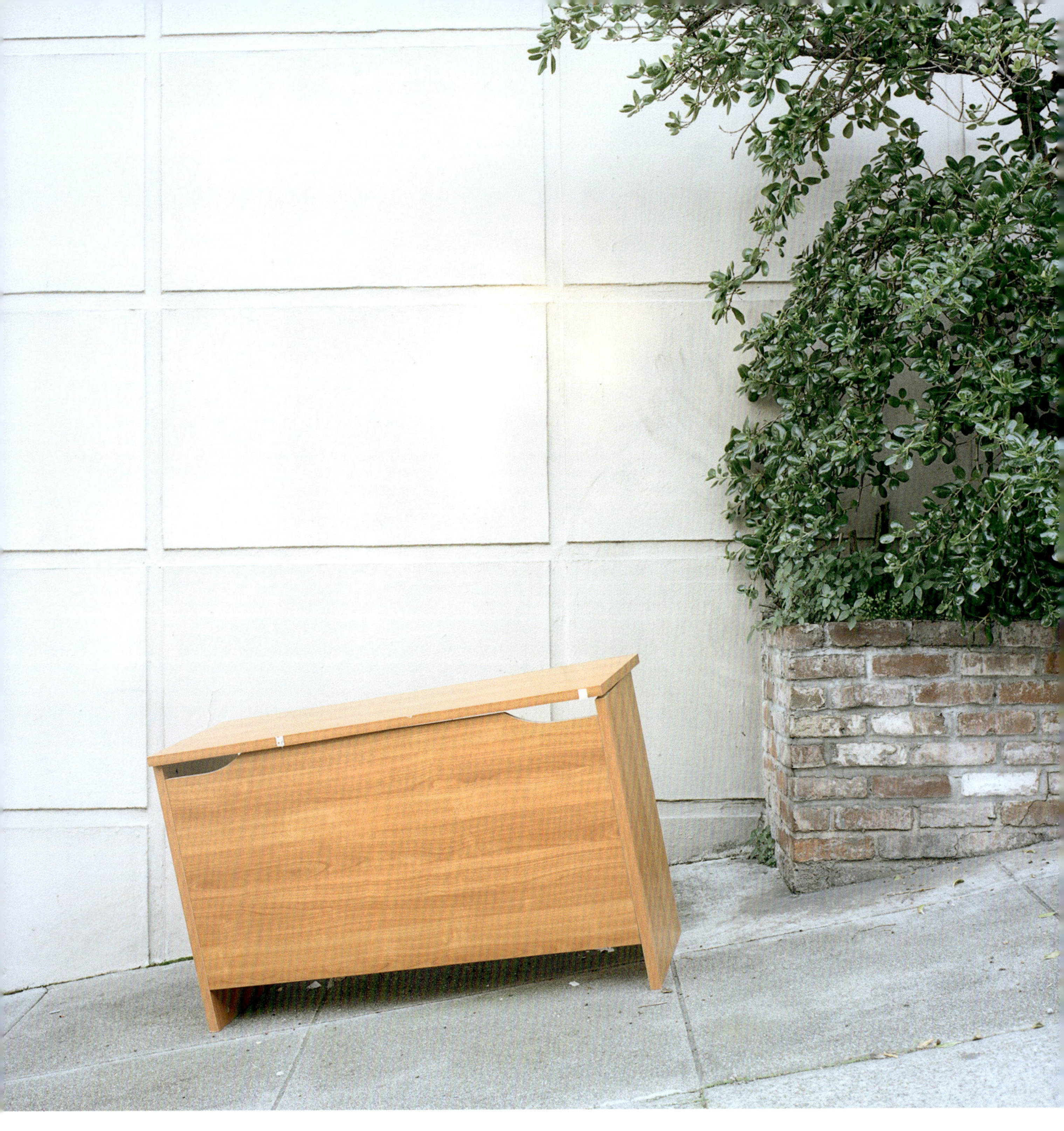

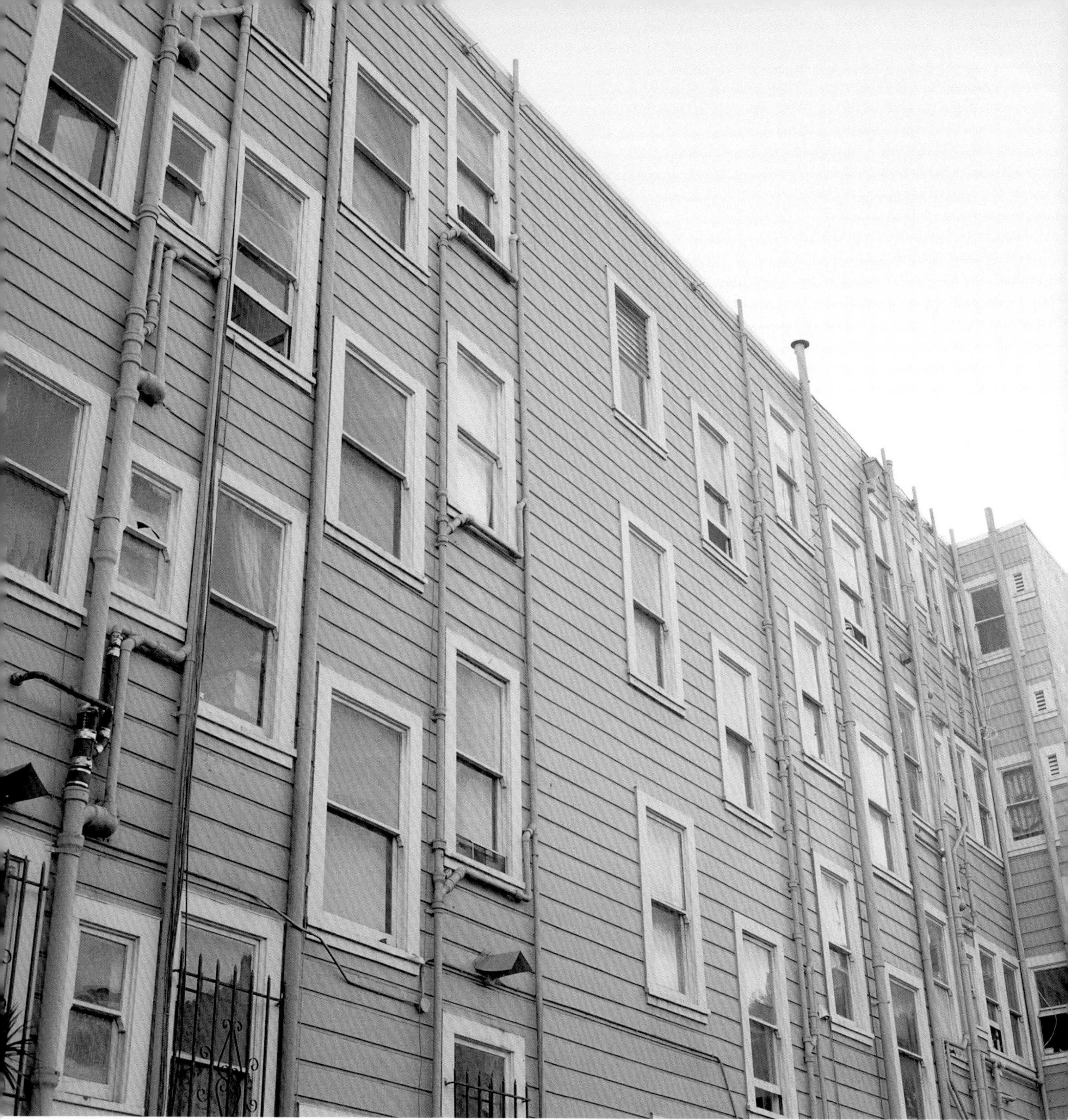

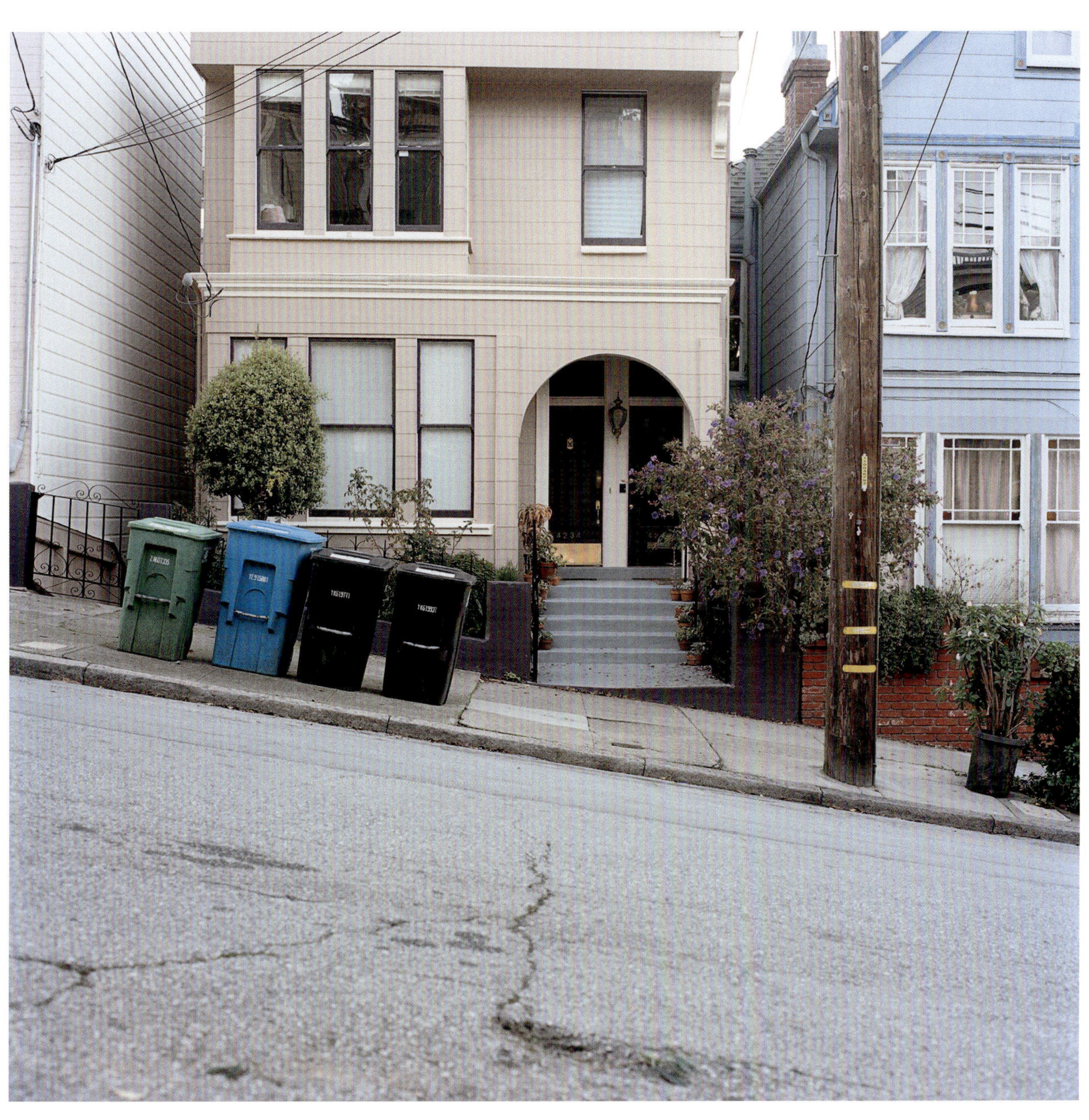
4234

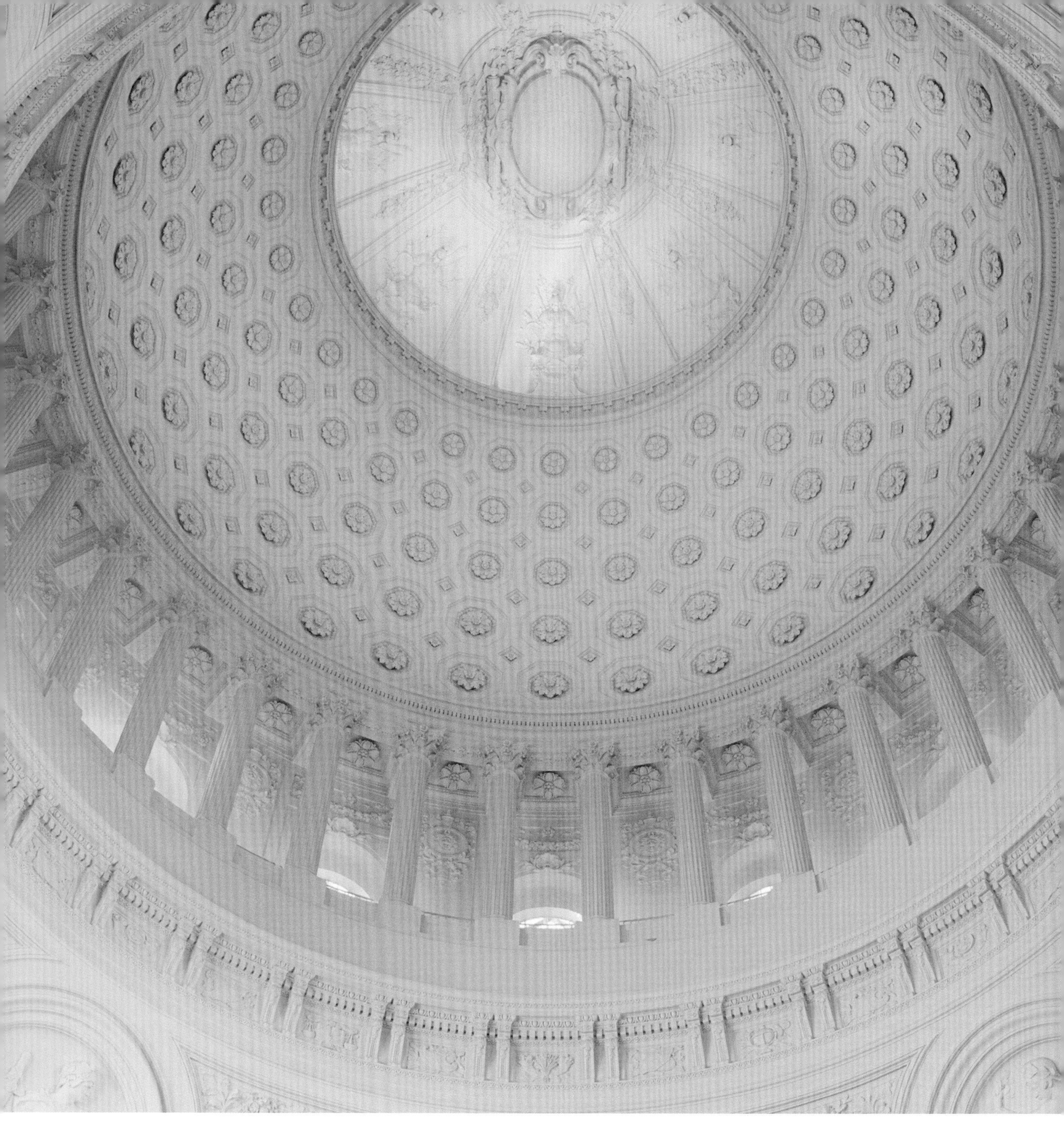

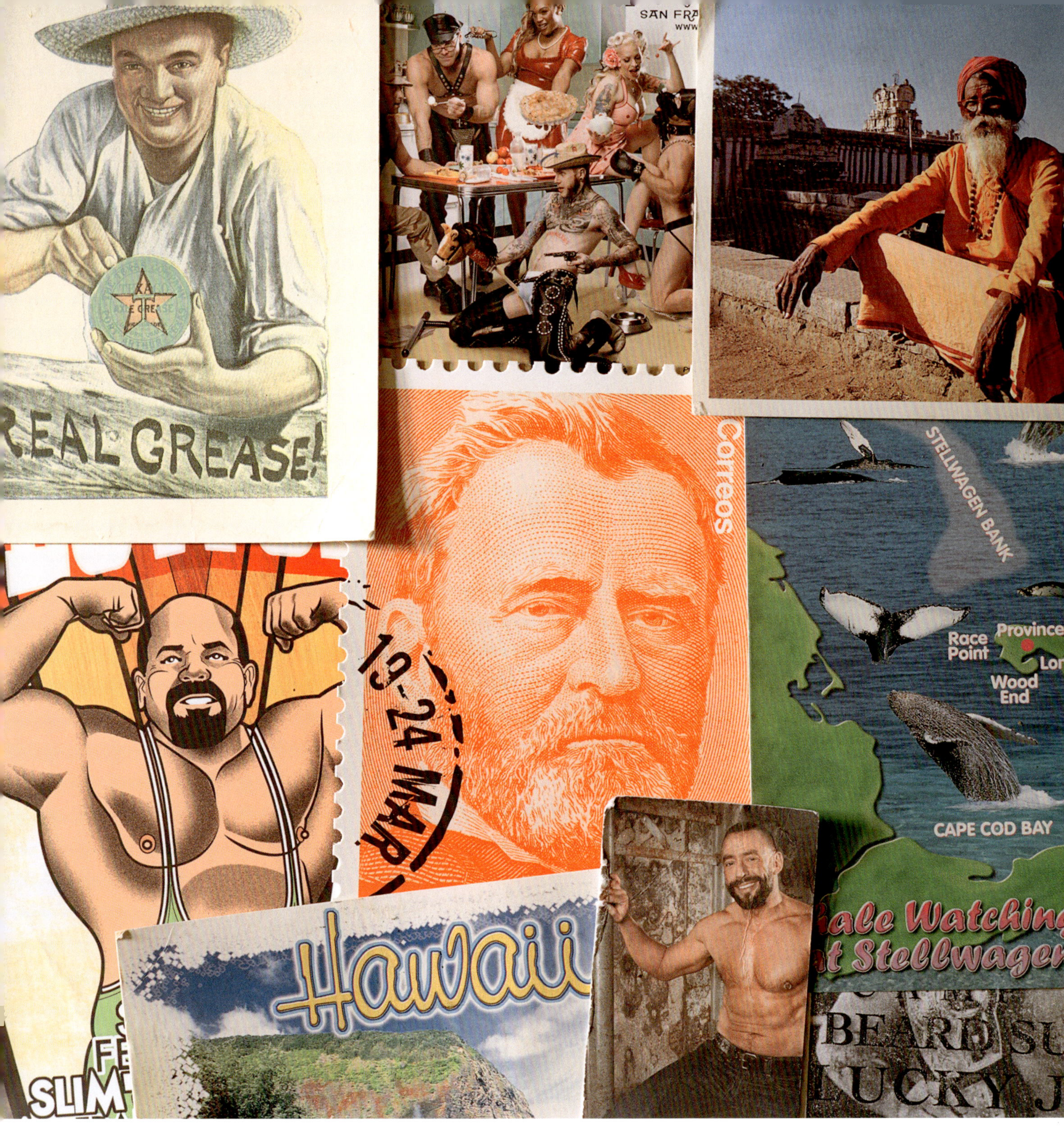
REAL GREASE!
SAN FRA
Correos
19-24 MAR
STELLWAGEN BANK
Race Point
Province
Wood End
CAPE COD BAY
ale Watching
at Stellwagen
Hawaii
BEARD SU
LUCKY J
SLIM

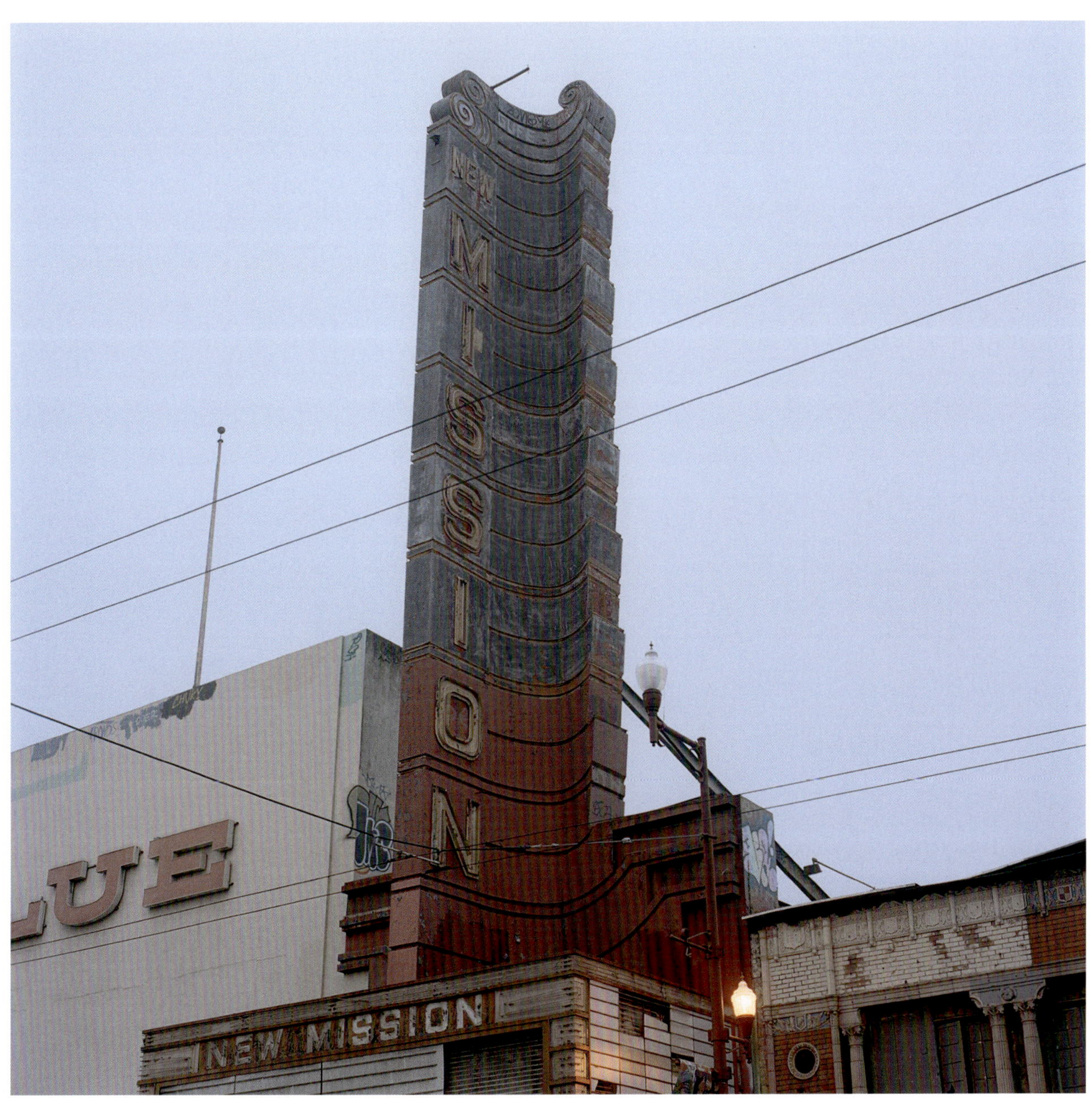
NEW
MISSION
LUE
NEW MISSION

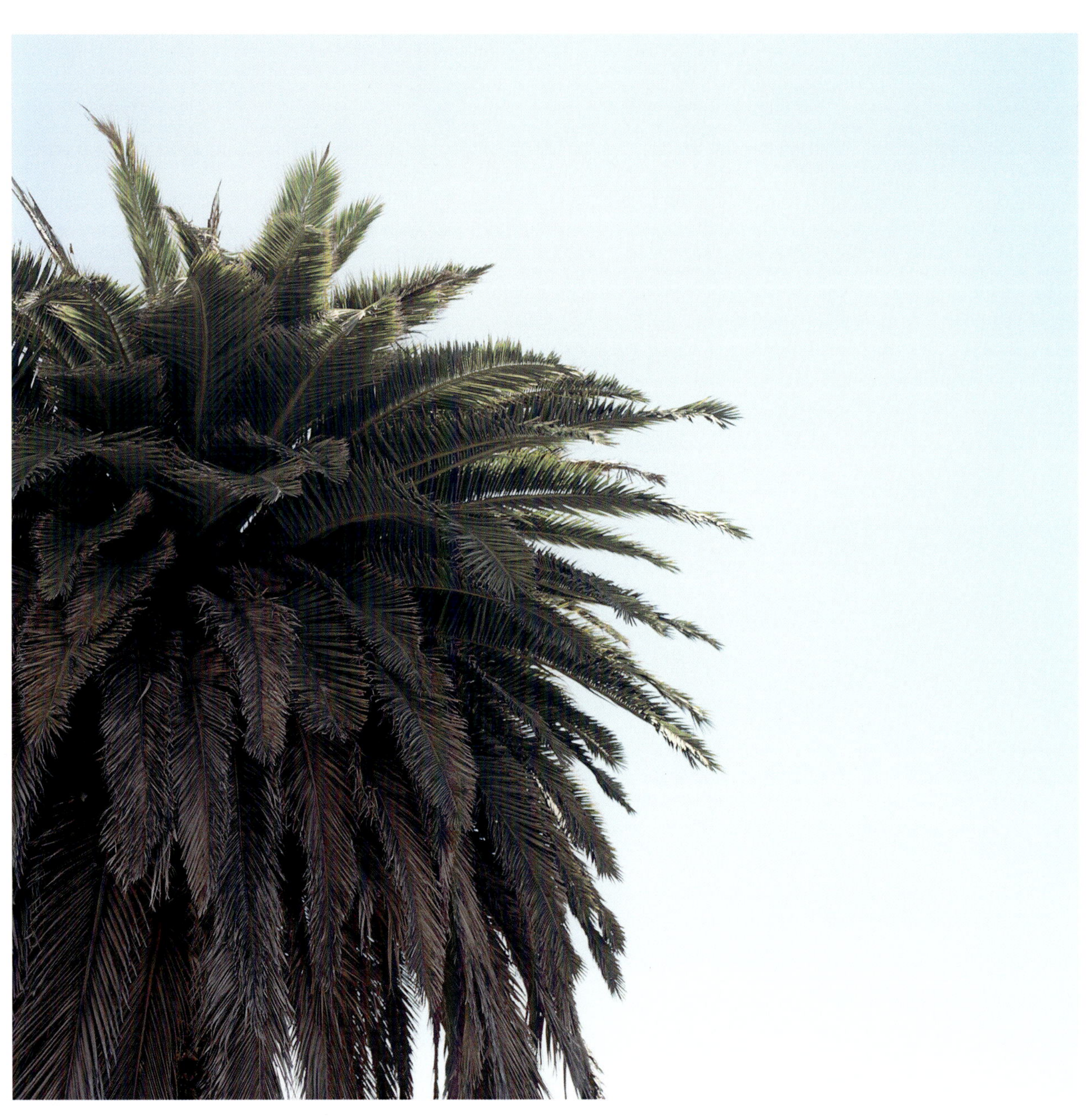

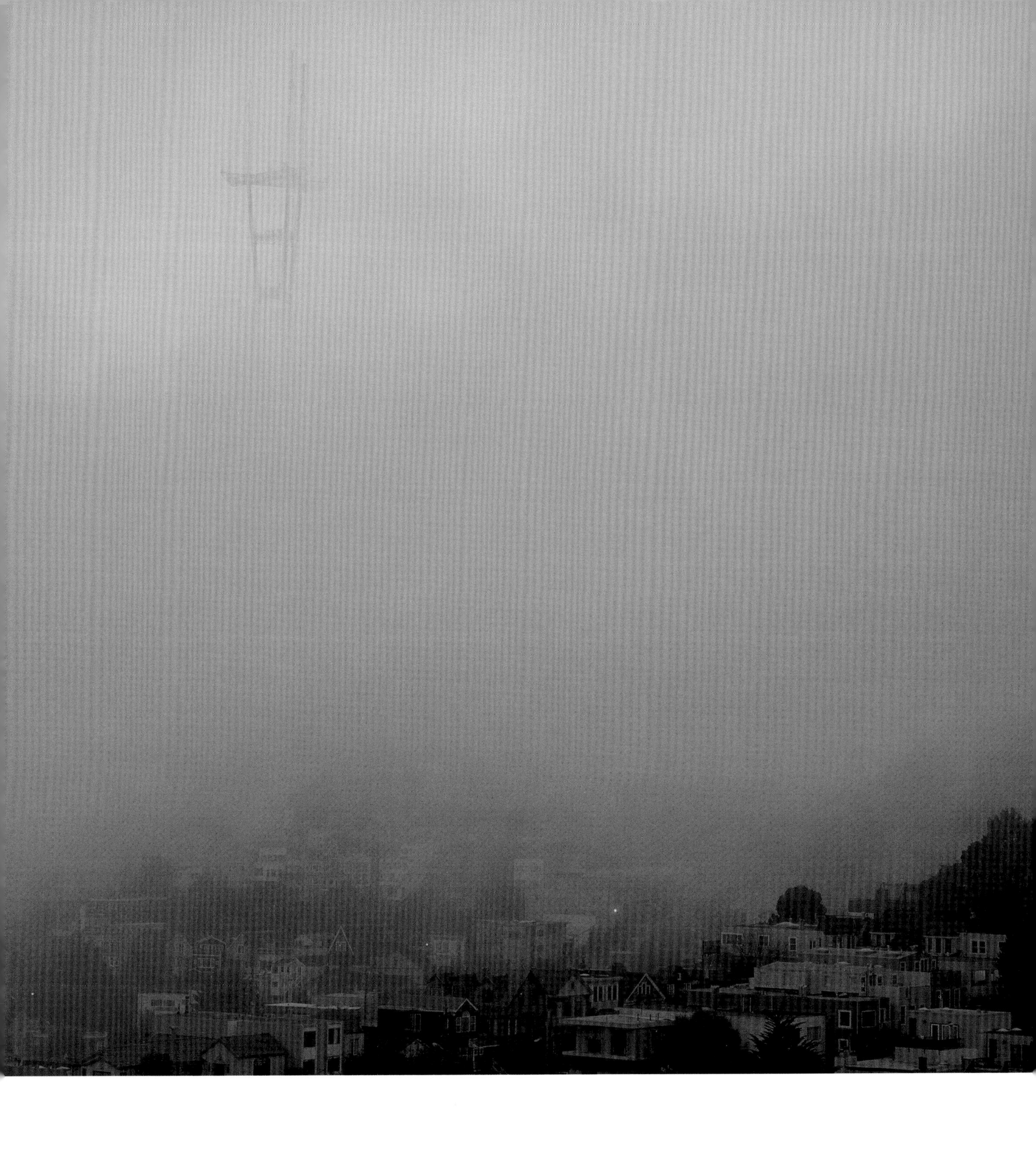

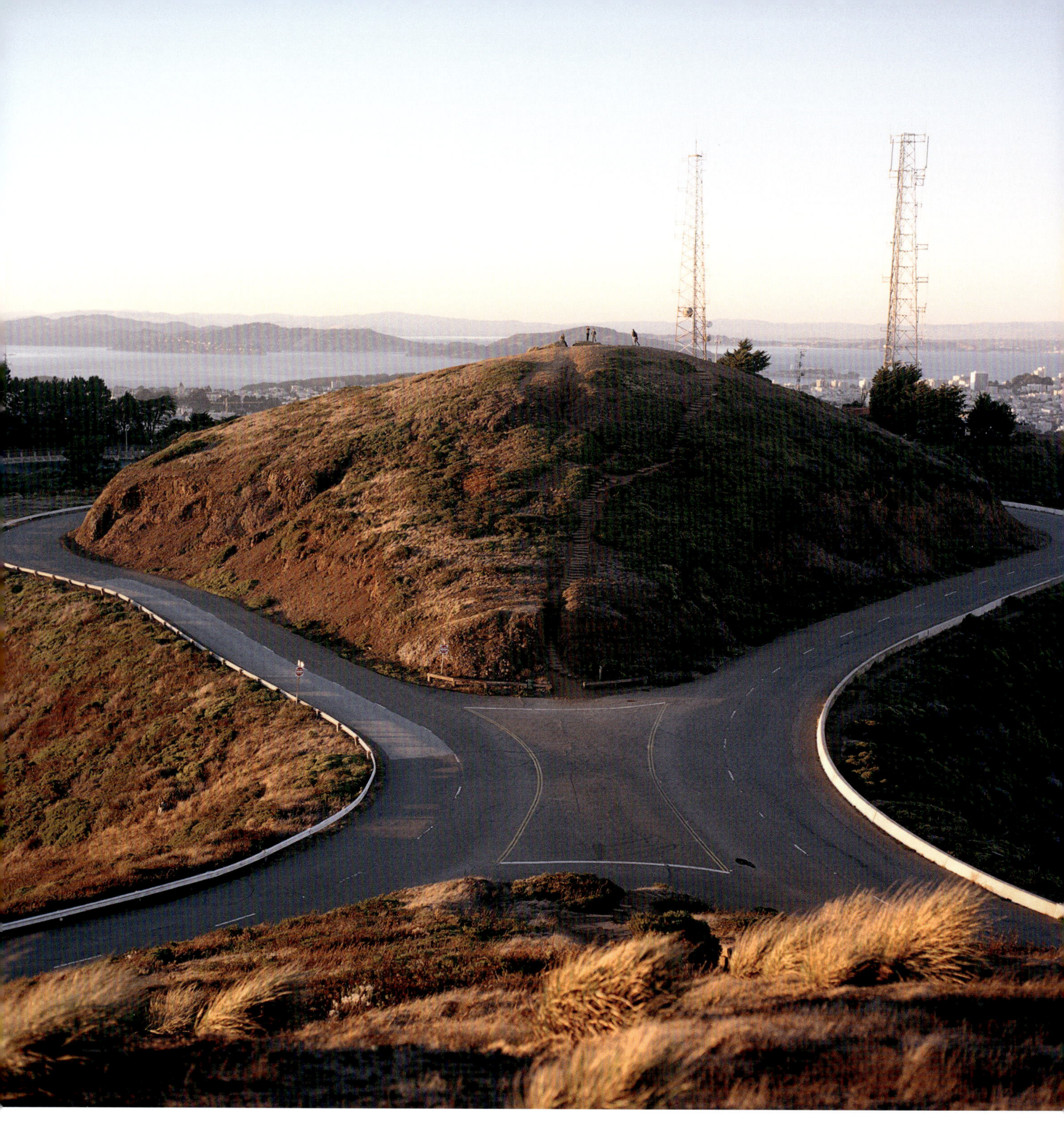

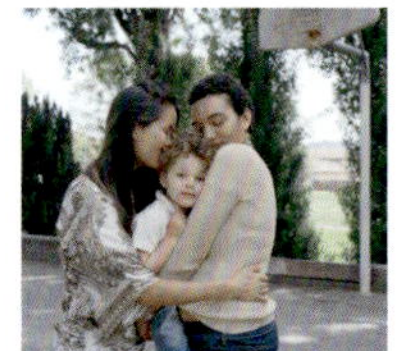

NYNKE, 34, HONG KONG
AIDAN, 3, CA
HEAVEN, 31, IL

EL CERRITO, MAY 2012

Karen is my heart's compass.——Karen is my home, my love and my life. We feel so very fortunate to have found each other and so very fortunate to still be together with a deep love and respect for each other, nurtured over twenty years.——Karen credits me with inspiring her and being a bright light for her? Well that's funny, since I feel the same way about her! I guess that is one of the reasons that we are together.——I have always been a bit *hardwired* to be analytical and pragmatic. Karen is less interested in [or driven by] practical matters and operates from a place of beauty and joy, in the moment. I used to describe *us* with an image of me, grounded, and Karen, floating up off the ground ... as she begins to float up past me I reach up and grab her ankle. In so doing, she pulls me up a bit off the ground and I keep her from floating up into the land of Tinkerbell!——Now, after listening to Karen for many, many years tell me that *I have a choice* about how I respond to anything in life, and after going through a number of extremely challenging health issues ... I've finally begun to *get it*. I've finally managed to really grasp the very simple lesson that Karen has tried to share with me – these moments are all we have. Literally, I can decide, even after having a horrendous muscle spasm in my back the night before this photo shoot and Karen and I dealing with a lot of sadness around death and loss in the months, weeks ... days before – I still can choose to, despite the pain and sadness, focus on the love and peace in my life and in this moment [especially with Karen!].——**Robin is my heart center**. She is like a bright light shining on the present, past and future for me.——My past did not include the word gay. There were no out role models and no discussions about being gay. I did not fit in and did not know why.——My present includes belonging to a family who votes for politicians and laws that aim to keep people like us second-class citizens. Gay rights seem so wrong to them. Robin provides me with the relief I need in a world full of hatred and fear. Her advocacy for human rights, compassion and learning consistently brings me hope. Her loving family [that I am now a part of] calls me their daughter-in-love [instead of daughter-in-law]. I finally feel like I belong.——I grew up in Southern California. Robin grew up in the San Francisco Bay Area. The cost of living is super high here in California, especially San Francisco, but we feel like it's worth it. We need the diversity and the open minds, which help us feel emotionally and physically safe.——As for the future, she inspires me to be a better person, living life fully with compassion, respect and truth.——Thank you Robin, for reading my personal ad in the East Bay Express and changing my life forever.

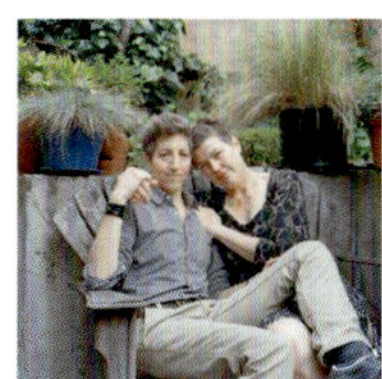

OAKLAND, APRIL 2012

KAREN, 50, CA
ROBIN, 50, CA

I became part of this family the moment I was born in 2002. My dog Porter became part of this family in 2011. I know for myself – and it's kind of obvious for Porter – that we are both very happy here. We love our family just the way it is.

TRAYLOR, 9, CA
J. MIKE, 60, TX
CHRIS, 49, TX

SAN FRANCISCO, APRIL 2012

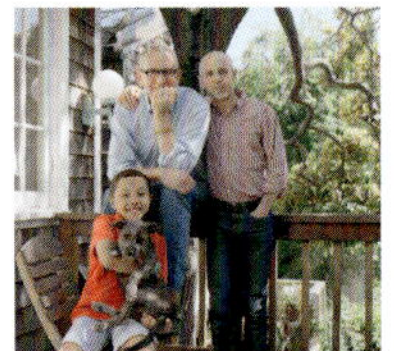

We are the ultimate San Francisco Bay Area blended family. When Lisa and I fell in love, we each had a child from a previous relationship, as well as the ups and downs of joint custody and half-siblings in other homes. Lisa, Ariel, Hannah and I understand that families evolve and grow – and that we're always lucky to have more people with whom we share our love.

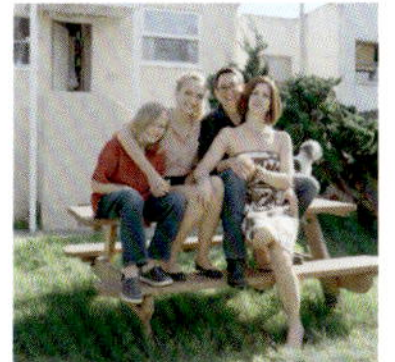

ALBANY, FEBRUARY 2012

ARIEL, 9, CA
HANNAH, 17, CA
LISA, 45, IL
LIBBY, 44, MI

»Making the decision to have a child is momentous.—It is to decide forever to have your heart go walking around outside your body.« [Elizabeth Stone]—The above quote epitomizes my feeling about my daughter Kaila. My heart not only wanders outside my body it wonders beyond my imagination. My imagination has grown tremendously in trying to keep Kaila engaged and dreaming of Life's possibilities.—As gay parents we certainly choose to take care of a Life and/or bring a new Life into this world. We were blessed to have the added bonus of Kaila being created by both my ex-partner and my brother. We are learning to become better parents everyday as Life brings its many challenges and keeps constantly changing. Kaila went from having two parents and our immediate family to a village of new partners, ex-partners, uncles, aunts and grandparents galore. In addition we have created family with our close friends and strongly feel that our community is just that a community of love, respect and joy.

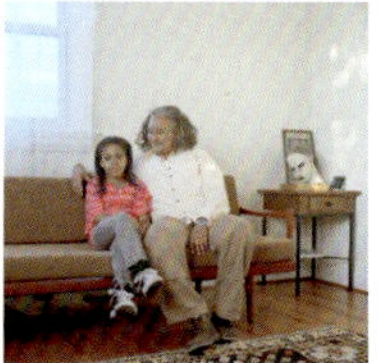

KAILA, 8, CA
DONNA, 51, TRINIDAD

OAKLAND, SEPTEMBER 2012

Being the Daddy I Never Had. As a child I was often reminded that my father had everything to do with our unfortunate impoverishment. His name was known by many, but only in the context of a rolling stone who slinks around downtown Louisville in his cardinal red El Dorado, vanishing like vapor before the results of a pregnancy test were revealed. When I return home I often meet a new half-brother or sister. They have the exact same story as I do. Meeting our father once or twice, around kindergarten age, receiving a gift [mine was Connect Four], patting our little afros, and then never seeing or hearing from him again. We were the southern bastard stereotypes.—Accountability for dads to be present in their children's lives, at least in the form of a child support check, was not a reality to me back then. Everything fell on my mother's shoulders. She gave birth to me at the age of 18, took three jobs, snuck me in and out of her apartment to avoid eviction. It is a rough job being a single African-American mother in America.—Upon discovering that I was going to be a father, I was just as excited as I was worried. I knew that even though it was an opportunity to reverse the *deadbeat dad* legacy of my father, I had absolutely no idea how to make it work. There was no example for me to follow or blueprint for reference. My child's mom and I were already thinking of separating, but I did not let it stop me from being in my daughter's life. I had always wanted to be a father. I loved my little girl and I love being a dad. I wanted to stay a part of her life and take care of her, so I did the broke parenting drill with a 21st century twist: as a single Mr. Mom; using our stroller to steal diapers from the pharmacy, happy to eat just once a day, begging the baby mama to pump more breast milk and being present in my baby's life as her queer African-American dad.—My queer identity is not the central point of my struggle as a parent. The heart of the dilemma is race. I feel persecuted for being a single African-American male parent, regardless of sexuality in our society. When people question how that cute bi-racial child could have actually sprung forth from my sissy loins, I simply tell them it is biology. When they assume I am straight, I tell them I am not boring enough for that. Humor keeps me going in that realm, but not when it comes to race.—After five years of so-called co-parenting with my daughter's mother, I sought mediation through the family court, and was finally able to find a fair joint custody schedule. I was also able to pursue full time work as a schoolteacher in California. The mother of my child responded by petitioning for child support. The court calculated that she deserved a monthly payment because she would begin to take care of our girl 5% more of the time than I would, even though she had a way better support network than I did.—It seems to me that the family court punishes all fathers, regardless of their situation, because of the standards set by deadbeat dads like my own. I was surrounded by them, and the only thing we had in common was our race. The court knew baby mama made more money than I, they knew her parents had paid for her house, while my name collected dust on a Section 8 wait list. They also knew that I had been with my little girl for most of the time up until that point, but it did not matter. I am an African-American dad in a custody battle. Being single and queer is simply icing on the cake.—As I came to find out, mothers are the entitled beneficiaries in this circumstance, not the children. So what do I do? Do I abandon my child in search of a better life free of systems that discriminate against me? Do I terrorize society, targeting those same institutions that abuse hard-working fathers such as myself? No. All I can do is keep on loving, and keep on fighting. To keep looking for community connections, even if some gay dads turn their nose up at me when I enter their turf, as if I just walked in from the Richmond Landfill. To keep moving forward even when I feel invisible to other fathers in San Francisco groups who tend to be married or working on it, white, at least ten years older than I, and typically wealthy enough to even consider adoption or other types of family formation. I can't allow negative experiences with privileged folks or discriminatory institutions to damage the support networks that I wish to create for my beautiful daughter.——I love my daughter to death. She's got a cartoon character's voice and smile that could melt a glacier. When we're alone on a Friday night, we have dance parties with just the two of us [and several stuffed animal VIPs]. She's also the loudest person I know. You could probably hear her whispering from a mile away. I've been there to see her take her first steps, say her first words, and lose her first tooth. I've loved every minute of it.——My daughter called me mama when she was just beginning to speak. She is my heart and she keeps me inspired to find new ways to parent. And I, her mama/daddy, learn each day that the measure of a man is determined, in reality, by how much [for lack of a better word] motherhood he's able to endure.

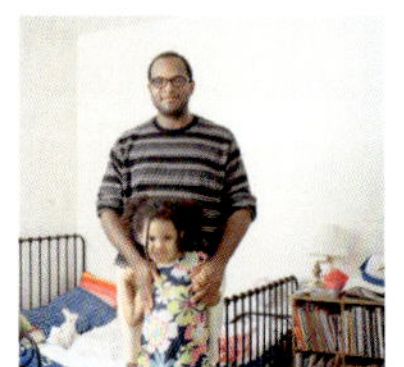

KAYEN, 5, ARGENTINA
DEWAYNE, 34, KY

OAKLAND, SEPTEMBER 2012

Illinoisans by birth, San Franciscans by choice. Thirty-five years together: 09/21/12

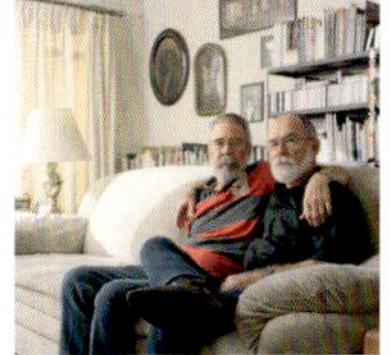

SAN FRANCISCO, NOVEMBER 2011

JIM, 59, IL
TERRY, 66, IL

We have been together through a lot of highs and lows in the last 10 years. We have so much fun in the good times and support each other through the tougher times. We love sharing our lives with the wonderful people and fabulous food of San Francisco.

MATT, 32, OH
PAUL, 32, MI

SAN FRANCISCO, NOVEMBER 2011

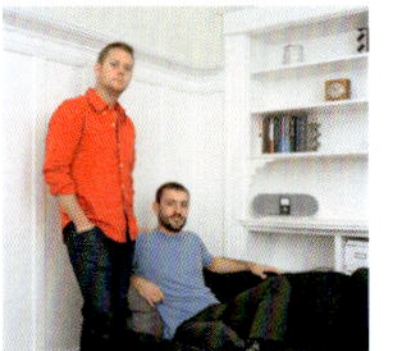

From the first time we met until now, 15 years later, our relationship has been much like our house remodel: a truly fun experience. They both evolve without excessively hard work. They challenge our gay creativity gene. And they both just feel so right, like a puzzle where all the pieces fit perfectly, and none are missing ... because WE get to custom make the pieces as we go!

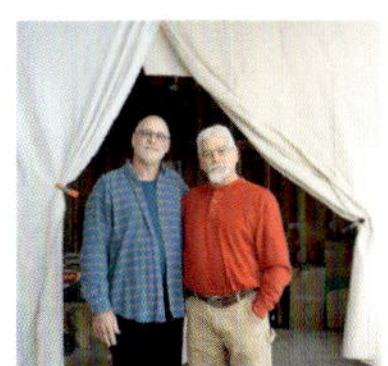

SAN FRANCISCO, NOVEMBER 2011

JEFF, 58, OH
CARL, 68, PA

We have been together for 8 years; 4 in Chicago and 4 in San Francisco. We both grew up in Chicago but we now call San Francisco our second home. I have never met anyone who makes me laugh, cry, get stronger, get weaker, believe, pursue my dreams, and love, the way she does. San Francisco is my physical home, but she is my *home*.

TOMOMI, 25, JAPAN
AUDREY, 27, IL

SAN FRANCISCO, SEPTEMBER 2012

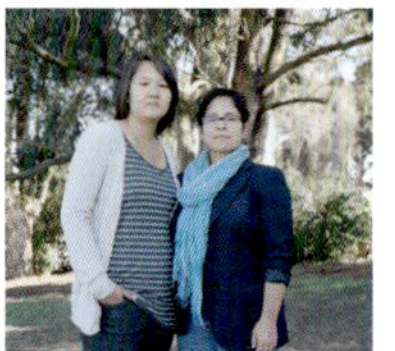

My whole world in two—Simply nothing to explain—Family is Joy

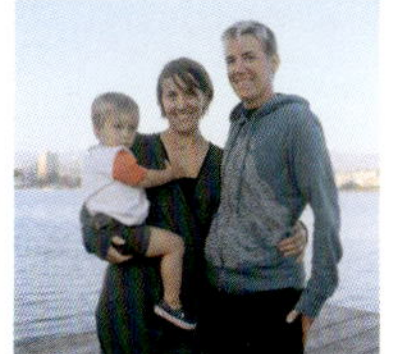

OAKLAND, SEPTEMBER 2012

RHONE, 1, CA
BRITTANY, 38, OR
CAROL, 47, WI

These photos were taken six years after we met, and three or four years into our marriage – four years if you're talking legal marriage; we took advantage of California's limited time offer for queer couples in 2008, but we gathered with friends and family for a more formal marriage ceremony/celebration and honey-moon a year later.——Daniel's lens keenly uncovers the Story of Us at this particular moment in time. Perhaps in contrast to most of the families represented in this beautiful volume, we've faced some tough challenges lately, but our son Bodhi [an intensely happy, resilient, curious *miracle child*, whose name – chosen even before he was conceived – suits him more than we'd ever imagined] brings us both immense joy. His presence in our lives calls on us to be our biggest selves and support each other through rough waters as we engage in this wondrous improvisation called life.

DUKE, 46, GA
BODHI, 10 MONTHS, CA
ANGELIQUE, 43, CA

SAN FRANCISCO, MAY 2012

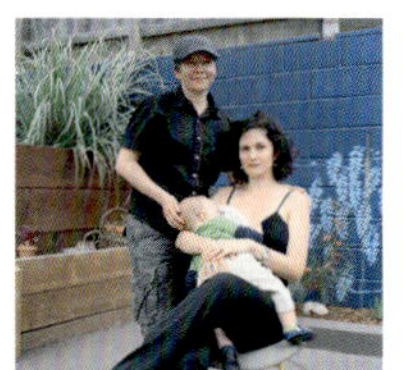

San Francisco has been our home for many years – Jim has lived here for nearly 25 years, Andrew was born here. Jim was attracted to *The City* by its beauty – the hills, the Victorian homes built side-by-side, the Bay and ocean, the many iconic landmarks including Coit Tower and the Golden Gate Bridge. Its legendary tolerance and the diversity of the people was also a great attraction for Jim as a not-yet-out gay man when he first moved here in the 1980's. Andrew left to go to school and work in Europe, but found his way back to the City by the Bay in 1989.——San Francisco helped Jim come to terms with his sexual orientation and he *came out* as a gay man a few years after he moved here. The openness of the local culture made it easy for him to live as an openly-gay man here even as American society as a whole has slowly struggled to accept its gay and lesbian citizens.——Andrew and Jim met at a Castro District cafe in San Francisco in 1989. It was pretty much *love at first sight* and has been a loving partnership ever since, with the inevitable ups and downs that any relationship experiences. They married at San Francisco City Hall in 2004 [before it was legal] and again in 2008 [before Proposition 8 again made it illegal].——San Francisco continues to be a place that allows them to live their lives and thrive as a married couple, finding joy in their relationships with friends, family, and certainly each other. They now share their home with their beautiful Golden Retriever, Diego, a rescue dog from Mexico.

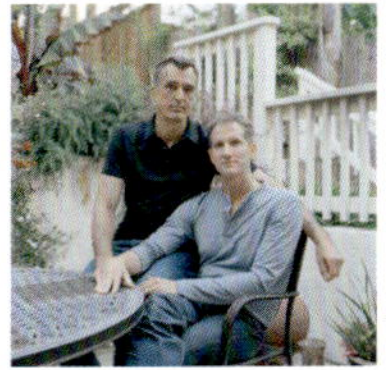

SAN FRANCISCO, MAY 2012

JIM, 51, WI
ANDREW, 46, CA

We met quite some time before we actually started dating. Something about those first encounters led us to stay in touch over several years. We maintained a tenuous connection via the occasional email to say hi or brief chat to ask how the other was doing. Various moves happened, other relationships came and went.——Eventually we reconnected in person and began to hang out. Neither of us was specifically looking for a relationship, and with Josh in San Francisco and Eric in Sacramento neither of us expected to end up together. So of course that's what happened, as both of us allowed the relationship to unfold and reveal itself.——Sometimes we spend more time in Sacramento, sometimes more time in San Francisco. The distance no longer bothers us, and the extra independence it affords can be a good thing at times. Perhaps someday we'll find ourselves together in one place. We can't predict what will happen, so we are enjoying and loving each other on the way there.

ERIC, 50, CA
JOSH, 31, CA

SAN FRANCISCO, APRIL 2012

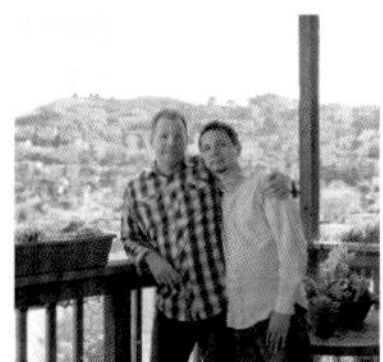

18th and Hattie will always hold a special place in our hearts. We have many memories spending happy moments with friends and family at that house in the corner and also on those sidewalks. We are not together, but we are currently working through our issues.

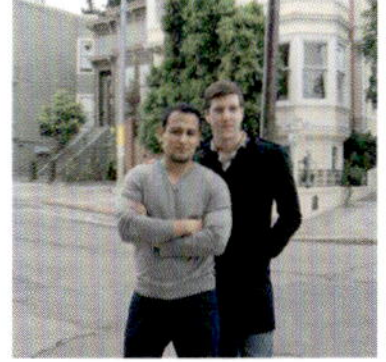

SAN FRANCISCO, NOVEMBER 2011

OMAR, 33, PERU
CEDRIC, 28, FRANCE

The moment that I was inseminated I knew that I was pregnant. Six weeks later, the test proved that I was in fact pregnant. Having sat around for years dreaming of my children I knew what his/her name was going to be. My pregnancy was a little difficult but it made me focus on my health and the health of my child. Our bond was formed already, I thought I was having a girl, but the sonogram pictures and legs wide open changed that, his name would be Javier. He came after 39 hours of labor, calm and awake. He's been here before, is what the wise ones would say upon meeting him, and he has. He is my soul.——My second pregnancy was a journey of months and months to years of trying. Right when I was going to give up, I got pregnant, my due date Javier's birthday. I told my second child, don't come on your brother's birthday he will never forgive you. He listened to my advice and came 5 days later, and that has been the last time he has taken my advice. Aluzio is my head strong child, he has to do things his way, and bend the world to him, not bend for the world. He is my heart.——My sons are my gift from GOD, my Heart and Soul and the LOVES of my life. They are ALL THAT MATTER.

JAVIER, 7, OH
JOY, 35, OH
ALUZIO, 3, CA

SAN FRANCISCO, OCTOBER 2012

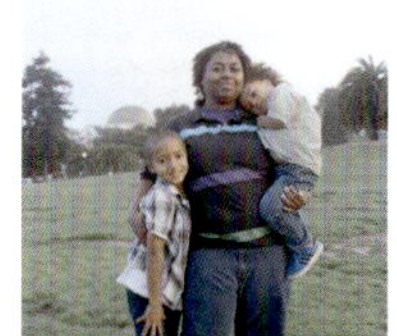

Both American-born with parents from China and Hong Kong, we met in the San Francisco Bay area and have been together for 16 years. Being great partners, we each took a turn at pregnancy, both from the same donor. Though we sometimes worry about how our kids will be treated by people who do not approve of our family, we are fortunate enough to live in a time and place where we mostly spend our time dealing with ordinary problems, such as getting the kids to eat their veggies and clean their room, and the challenges of fitting in work, school, activities, and play. We are grateful that the support of our family and friends, our kids' teachers, and our surrounding community, allows us to be, well, ordinary.

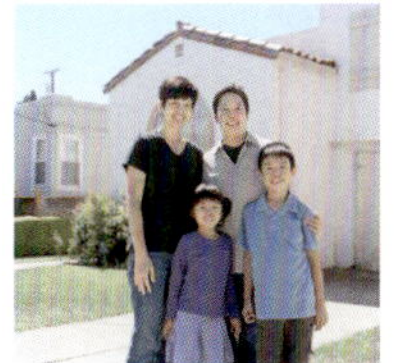

BERKELEY, SEPTEMBER 2012

DIANE, 43, HI
JING, 5, CA
DAO, 43, MD
TAI, 8, CA

We have been partners for 10 years, and we are in the process of adopting Nia through the San Francisco foster care system. We are so excited about being mommies, it is truly a dream come true.——Our family is a patchwork quilt. Each of us is a whole, beautiful, unique fabric – we each represent different cultures, ethnicities, and life stories. When sewn together, we create a striking and complex quilt, each piece remaining unaltered and existing in its own right. Together, our patchwork quilt illuminates the beauty and vibrancy that is a modern day family.

ELANA, 33, CA
NIA, 5 MONTHS, CA
MARLENE, 36, CA

OAKLAND, AUGUST 2012

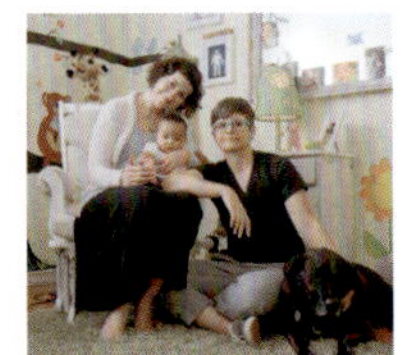

Through love, blossoms love.

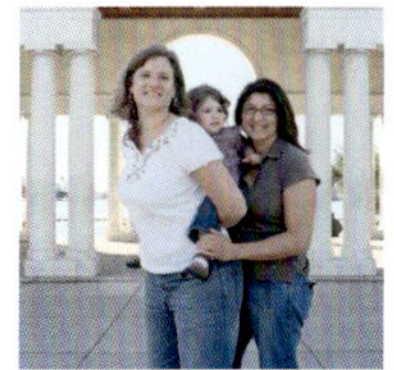

OAKLAND, JANUARY 2012

AMY, 42, NY
GENEVA, 2, CA
YVONNE, 44, CA

They say, »when it's right, you know it.« But I didn't know the meaning until now. I now have my soul mate, and the days are brighter than ever before. Even the hard times are easier with her beside me.——More than two decades later, together with our lovely daughter and our two adorable puppies, we continue on this precious journey called life, all the while counting our blessings that we are a family.

LORNA, 51, KENYA
CHRISTINA, 22, CA
LYNETTE, 57, PAKISTAN

WALNUT CREEK, SEPTEMBER 2012

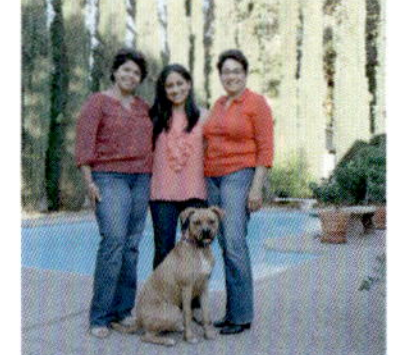

We met 7 years ago became friends and found out that we have a great deal in common. Born in the same hospital in Vermont, going to the same graduate school in the Midwest and finally landing on the same block clear across the United States 38/45 years later. Art, food, the outdoors, community service, real estate, health and wellness, family, friends, travel and fashion serve as common interests in our lives. We both are committed to enjoying our life individually and as a couple and leaving our community in better shape as a result of our having been here. The San Francisco Bay Area allows our interests to be broad and deep and we are grateful to have the opportunity to live here with one another and our trusted companion Jake.

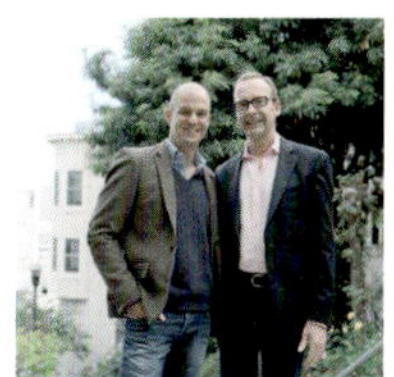

SAN FRANCISCO, SEPTEMBER 2012

PETER, 44, VT
TIM, 52, VT

JUDY, 47, OH
CHERYL, 54, MI

OAKLAND, JANUARY 2013

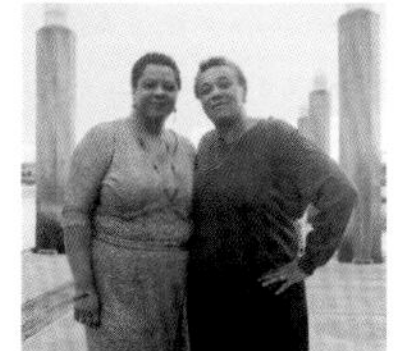

We met online in December 2002, when Sigi answered an ad Lisa posted on Craigslist for »just a New Year's Eve date.« We felt an instant connection and have been a couple ever since our first date. We were married at our synagogue before family and friends on the Hebrew calendar date of 19 Elul 5764 [2004], and a second time on 19 Elul 5766 [2006] during the brief window of time when same-sex marriages were legal in California. Lisa's two children live with us. Sigi's two daughters live elsewhere.——When we met, Lisa's daughter was 7 and her son was 11, so Sigi has been a significant part of their lives for most of their childhoods. We see ourselves as an ordinary family with a house and kids and dogs and all of the challenges and rewards that come with raising children and building a strong extended family.——We both grew up in the Bay Area and we love living in Oakland. This city has made it easy for each of us to be part of a warm and diverse community – our friends are not exclusively gay or straight, nor are they exclusively Philippino or Puerto Rican [like Sigi] or Mexican or Ashkenazi [like Lisa]. We are both out at our jobs and in our religious community. Our families are uneven in their acceptance of our relationship, but the love and support from our extended family and the deep love we have for each other has more than made up for that.

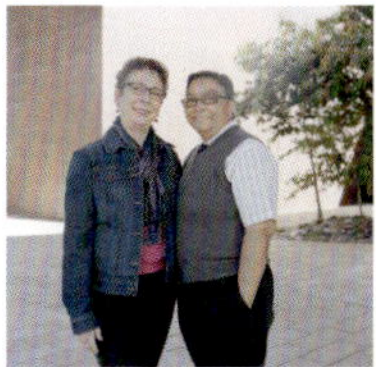

SAN FRANCISCO, MAY 2012

LISA, 57, CA
SIGI, 56, CA

We didn't want to be parents. In fact, we made a decision early in our relationship that things were perfect with us and our two dogs and that was everything we needed.—But all that changed.—Suddenly, our friends were becoming parents and we were starting to reconsider our decision. We didn't dicsuss this with each other. Rather, it was a silent, internal discovery we were each making about ourselves.—One afternoon, after a particularly harrowing day including unruly children, running out of gas and extreme hunger, we sat down at a restaurant. Each at the end of our ropes, I turned to Steve and said; »I think I want to have kids.«—Naturally, this was a big statement given our decision not to have kids.—He sat for a moment and considered the statement. Then he looked at me with conviction – and maybe a little fear – and said; »I do too.«—That was nine years into our relationship. It took another two before we found Robert and then another four to find Ray. I tell the boys all the time that we were looking for them and are so glad that someone kept them safe until we arrived and now that they are ours, we'll never let them go.—I say this all the time about parenting; It's harder than I thought but better than I thought.

STEVE, 51, MN
ROBERT, 10, CA
RAYMOND, 5, CA
DANNY, 45, NJ

SAN FRANCISCO, JUNE 2012

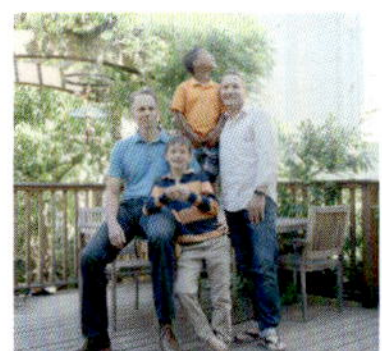

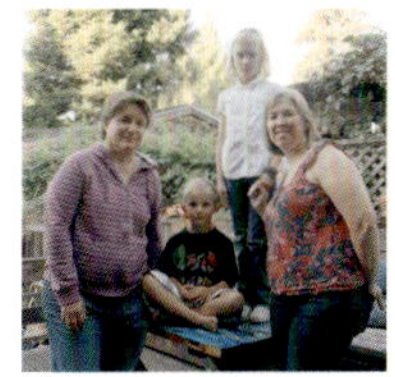

BERKELEY, SEPTEMBER 2012

SARAH, 49, CA
AMON, 5, CA
MAIZIE, 8, CA
JEN, 39, TX

Our first date: a perfect picnic in Dolores Park

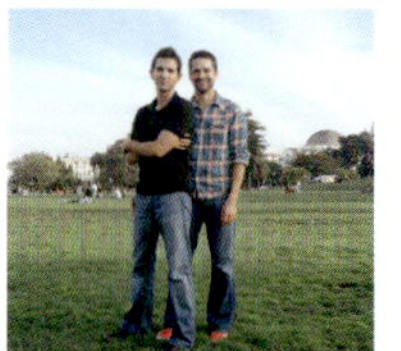

JARED, 27, TX
MICHAEL, 33, NY

SAN FRANCISCO, NOVEMBER 2011

Lotus and I met at the tail end of 1997 and instantly fell in love. We were married [though not legally] in 1999. A few years ago, our relationship hit a rough patch, and we broke up. It was the darkest time of both our lives. We were apart for four years, but never truly separated. Through new relationships and new homes, we remained connected. Finally, perhaps inevitably, we got back together, and our relationship is stronger and happier than ever.

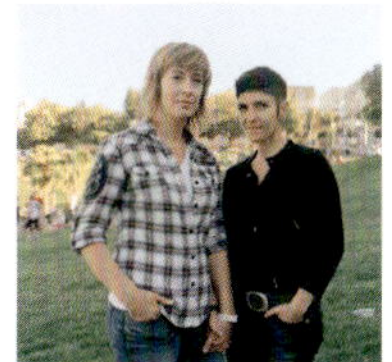

SAN FRANCISCO, SEPTEMBER 2012

LOTUS, 43, OR
JENN, 41, MA

We met on an API [Asian Pacific Islander] lesbian and transgender community weekend get away in Tahoe in January. We made blueberry mickey mouse pancakes together for the whole cabin. At one point, I challenged Cat to eat a whole bag of sliced apples and she did. Cat taught me how to play Pai Gow the first night. The following night, we all played poker and Cat swept the table and promptly lost it all at the casino the next morning. It was a great weekend!

CAT, 29, OR
YUN, 32, CHINA

BERKELEY, AUGUST 2012

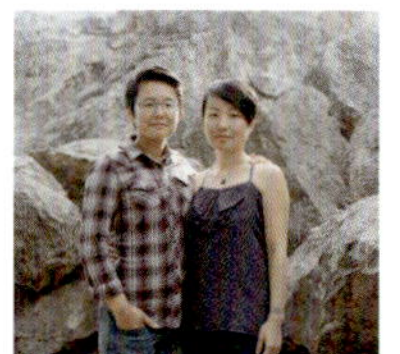

I am thankful that on November 13, 2010, I surrendered my fears, insecurities and questions to the Lord and chose to embark on a spiritual, emotional, intellectual, physical and romantic relationship with my best friend. Thank you Jesus!

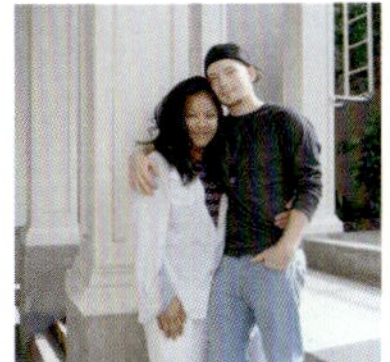

SAN FRANCISCO, MAY 2012

JOSEPH, 32, PHILIPPINES
SETH, 21, CO

We'll be successful!

TRINITY, 24, VIETNAM
NUT, 28, THAILAND

DALY CITY, MAY 2012

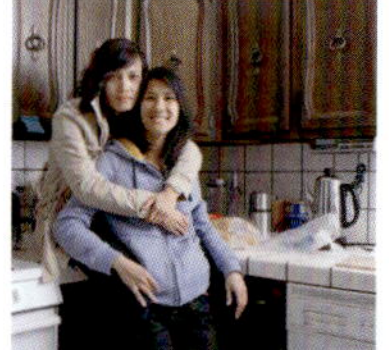

We're very lucky. We live in San Francisco where it's easy to be gay. In fact, I sometimes forget that we're any different from the straight couples we meet and hang out with.——It wasn't always this way for us, of course. We both grew up in the 70's – me in a small town in Louisiana and Sal in a more conservative, Sicilian family in New York. Being gay wasn't an option for either of us. No one discussed it and the only thing you ever heard about it was in derogatory terms.——So, like many of my gay friends, I learned to adapt by keeping myself private and hidden. It was a way to survive until you could get out and get to a safe place.——Now we're married and my life is better than I ever dreamed it could be. We're not only safe, we're better than safe. We're happy. And we're thriving. I sometimes shake my head at the wonder of it all ...

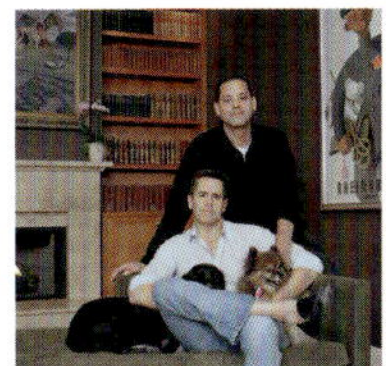

SAN FRANCISCO, NOVEMBER 2011

TOM, 47, LA
SAL, 48, NY

For more than a quarter of a century we have been on an incredible journey to build our life partnership.—We participated in creating a non-traditional extended family in which to have a child. We paid the cost of pioneering. We continue to reap the joys of parenthood. We raised an amazing son who, as a young adult, is bringing his creative energy to the world in the form of music.—We have worked hard in our respective fields – one of us supporting research of some of the most promising scientists from around the globe; one of us as a human rights activist and social justice educator. We have been active members of our communities – familial, professional, social, political.—We have built a loving, comfortable home where each of us has lived longer than any other place in our lifetimes. We have lived with numerous pets who have been members of our family. We have planted gardens and been nourished by their beauty as well as their fruits. We have been the caretakers of the small grove of Redwood trees that grace our yard.—We have traveled together. We have traveled separately. We have worked on joint projects. We have followed our separate creative pursuits – through voice and photography, music and art, gardening and cooking.—We have lived through many historical transitions. And we have been part of making history. We were married in 2004, a short-lived legal union that was invalidated within the same year. We were married again in 2008, a legal union that remains valid today as we continue the struggle for full equality.—And for more than twenty-six years we have shared, and expressed, and deepened our love of each other. For more than a quarter of a century we have been on an incredible journey to build our life partnership.

BARRY, 61, CA
MICHAEL, 64, CT

OAKLAND, JANUARY 2012

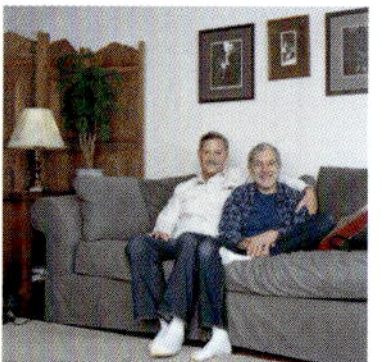

I can't think of a better place for us to raise our kids than San Francisco, a community so diverse that we have never felt out of place or different as a gay family. Our children can count among their peers with really varied family structures – one dad, two dads, one mom, two moms, traditional families with a mom and dad, grandparents raising grandchildren and even two moms and two dads. From the first week we moved here 12 years ago, San Francisco has felt like home. As much as any place can, it inspires us to live openly and proudly, and with compassion for others.

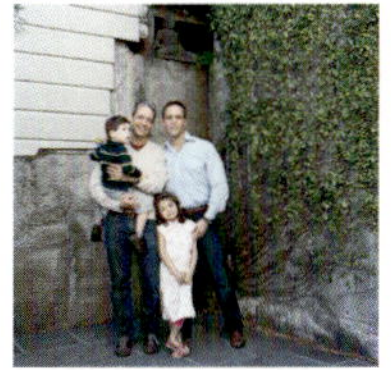

SAN FRANCISCO, FEBRUARY 2012

JESSE, 3, CA
JAY, 46, NC
AVERY, 6, CA
CRAIG, 43, NY

We're just like any other family – arguing; laughing; driving the kids to dance class, friends house, doctors appointments; feeding the cat; making dinner; rushing to get to work and school in the morning; doing laundry and more laundry; falling asleep early on Friday nights; but most of all, loving each other.

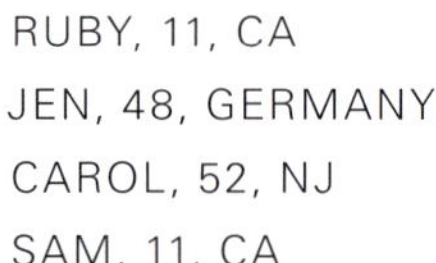

RUBY, 11, CA
JEN, 48, GERMANY
CAROL, 52, NJ
SAM, 11, CA

SAN FRANCISCO, SEPTEMBER 2012

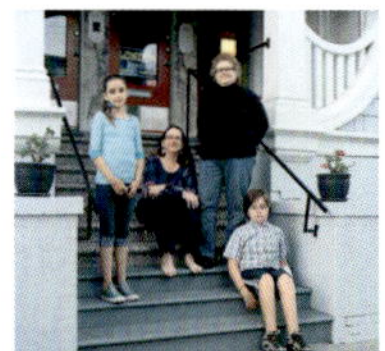

We are Emma, Audy, Jim and Michael. Jim and Michael have been a couple for 15 years, domestic partners for 12 and we married in 2008 during a brief period when California same-sex couples had the right to marry. We adopted Emma in 2003 and Audy in 2006. Having children is the best decision either of us has ever made. Our daughters are simply amazing and we love being parents. We also love living in the San Francisco Bay Area and realize how lucky we are to live in this *bubble* of sanity where our family is supported and celebrated.

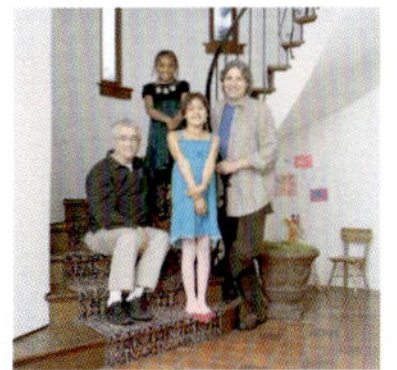

SAN FRANCISCO, JUNE 2012

JIM, 61, IA
AUDY, 6, CA
EMMA, 9, CA
MICHAEL, 57, PA

JOHN, 49, MN
MATTY, 2, PA

SAN FRANCISCO, JULY 2012

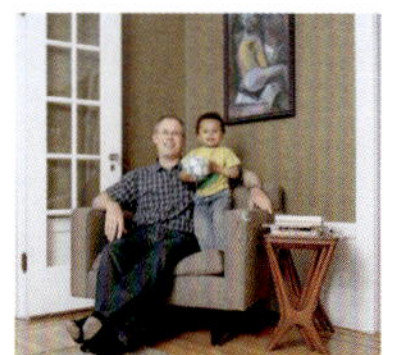

Wanting to have a child was one of the shared aspirations that drew Greg and me together from the earliest days of our romance. We both had supportive, loving families, and we both placed a high value on building a family of our own. Then, at our wedding in DC, Greg's sister offered to help us have a child. Thanks to this gift, our daughter shares a heritage from both sides of our family. She brings an energy and spirit to our lives that makes us thankful for her presence every single day.

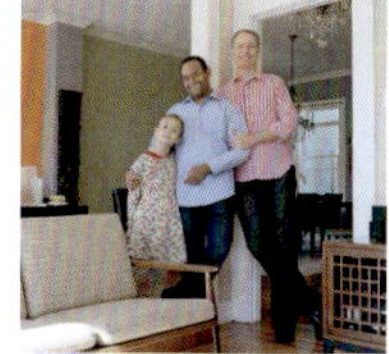

SAN FRANCISCO, JUNE 2012

CAROLINE, 7, PA
GREG, 43, CA
DAN, 47, PA

Dave and I have been together nearly eleven years. We discussed adoption on our first date. We both wanted a family. We found our son Zac five years ago. Then in January 2011 we found Nicky, a ten year old boy who needed a family. Zac, although concerned about sharing his dads, was fine with adopting Nicky because, »we have to save him, like you and Dadio saved me.« We adopted Nicky nine months after he was placed in our home, almost three years after we had adopted Zac. Now, we are looking for son number three and both Zac and Nicky are fully engaged in the search. We live in the hills north of Berkeley, but spend summers on our boat on Lake Shasta, a beautifully picturesque region of Northern California, where Zac comes from. I was born in Costa Rica. Dave was born in Indiana. Nicky is the only San Franciscan in this modern family. We met on match.com and fell in love on our first date!

NICKY, 12, CA
ARTURO, 47, COSTA RICA
DAVE, 42, IN
ZAC, 16, CA

EAST RICHMOND HEIGHTS, OCTOBER 2012

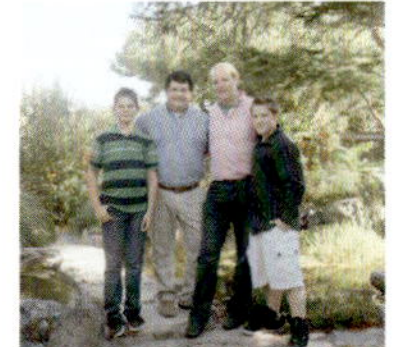

San Francisco is a special city to us both, not only as the gay capital of North America but it's also midway between our families in Iowa and New Zealand. We first met here 9 years ago and dated long distance across the Pacific between Sydney and here. After 18 months and a large carbon footprint we moved into our current home in the Castro district.——Living in San Francisco is amazing because it has a long history of activism and progressive politics for social rights for the gay community. It is important to both of us that our relationship is acknowledged by our friends, our family, and our immediate community. Everyone, from the dry cleaner to the corner grocer, acknowledge us as a couple, respect us and treat us like any other couple. We are grateful to live in a city that is so supportive of the gay community.

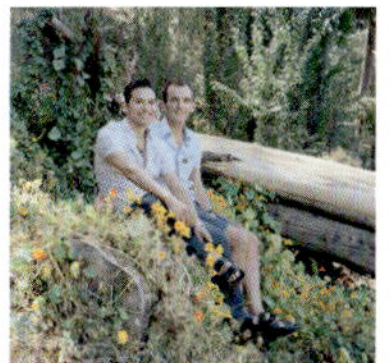

SAN FRANCISCO, JULY 2012

ALBERTO, 38, TX
STUART, 47, NEW ZEALAND

We met over 7 years ago in Washington DC and our adventures have never stopped. Each year together brings new challenges, new travels and new experiences. Our ancestries may have originated from vastly different cultural spaces, but our commitment and devotion to each other have overshadowed any obstacles. The truth is simply, we make each other a better person.

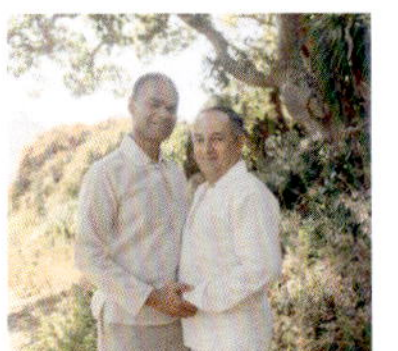

NEIL, 46, KENYA
ANDRES, 46, VENEZUELA

SAN FRANCISCO, AUGUST 2012

Our photo nicely reflects the deep love and passion that exploded between us when we first met, and lives on four years later. We are proof that there is such thing as *love at first sight* and that love is love regardless of who it is between. While we enjoy sharing our growing pride in being gay; marriage has brought into focus the wounds born of shame that we bring to our relationship as gay men who grew up in a bigoted intolerant society. We look to our love as the vehicle to heal the past, further deepen and strengthen our bond, and to gain the full self acceptance that was always our birthright.

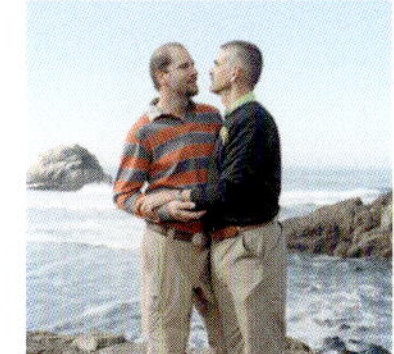

SAN FRANCISCO, NOVEMBER 2011

KEITH, 51, NJ
PHIL, 37, IN

BILL, 37, CA
CLAY, 51, CT

SAN FRANCISCO, MARCH 2012

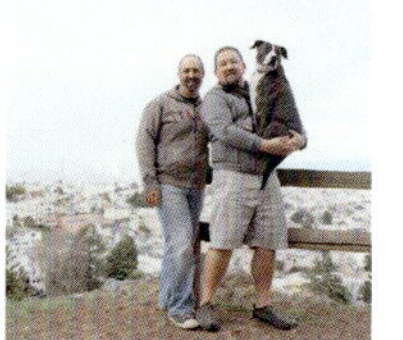

Peter and David are happily at home with Domino [their cat] sleeping on the couch under a picture of Monterey's Lone Cypress! They will celebrate their 35th anniversary in March 2013!

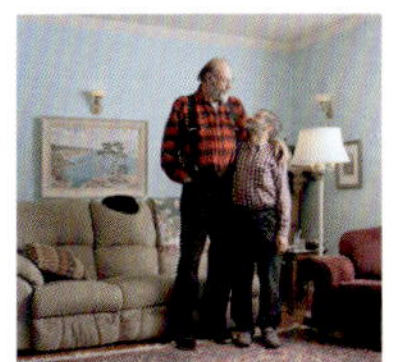

SAN FRANCISCO, NOVEMBER 2011

DAVID, 65, CANADA
PETER, 63, NY

ACKNOWLEDGEMENT

I want to thank all the wonderful couples and families whose pictures I have taken for the present book for their trust, their time, and their amazing texts. Furthermore, I want to thank *The German-American Fulbright Commission, Our Family Coalition,* the *Asian Pacific Islander Queer Women and Transgender Community,* and the *San Francisco LGBT Community Center* for their great support of my work.

I'm grateful to everybody who supported my project with their advice and action, especially my professors at the *Academy of Art University*, San Francisco, and *Folkwang University of the Arts*, Essen, Gisela Bullacher, Erik Butler, Will Mosgrove, Christopher Muller, Elisabeth Neudörfl, Elke Seeger, and Jim Sienkiewicz, as well as Clarissa Becker, Sarah Berger, Danny Buskirk, Dustin Delaney, Dirk Fütterer, Yaser Kaissy, Thomas Kellner, Luis Lopez, Rick Mordesovich, Marcus Pietrek, Sibylle Pietrek, Cesar Rodriguez, Robert Schlotter, Edith Schumann, Brigitta Sundermann-Spies, Wolfgang Vetten, Arne Vogt, and Udo Zinram.

I want to thank Christina Leber for her preface.

For their generous support, I want to thank the *Kerber Verlag,* the *Hörmann Group,* Dr. Constanze Paffrath, and Hasso von Blücher.

A personal thank you goes to Carla Crawley, my wonderful woman, for her great advice and her loving support.

IMPRINT

Images, Concept, and Design Daniel Schumann
Editors Daniel Schumann, Christof Kerber
Mentoring Elisabeth Neudörfl, Jim Sienkiewicz
Preface Christina Leber
Texts The People
Translation of the preface Karen Williams
Project Management, Kerber Verlag Martina Kupiak

Printed and published by Kerber Verlag, Bielefeld
Windelsbleicher Straße 166–170
33659 Bielefeld
Germany
Phone +49.521.9500810
Fax +49.521.9500888
info@kerberverlag.com

Kerber, U.S. Distribution
D.A.P., Distributed Art Publishers, Inc.
155 Sixth Avenue, 2nd Floor
New York, NY 10013
United States of America
Phone +1.212.627.1999
Fax +1.212.627.9484

The publication of this book has been generously supported by the *Kerber Verlag*, the *Hörmann Group*, Dr. Constanze Paffrath, and Hasso von Blücher.

The *Deutsche Nationalbibliothek* lists this publication in the *Deutsche Nationalbibliografie*; detailed bibliographic data are available on the Internet at http://dnb.dnb.de.

Kerber publications are available in selected bookstores and museum shops worldwide [distributed in Europe, Asia, South and North America].

First Edition
Printed in Germany

ISBN 978-3-86678-873-2
www.kerberverlag.com

A Collector's Edition of four images [13.75 x 13.75 inches each, chromogenic color prints] signed by Daniel Schumann has been published. This edition is limited to five copies and one artist's proof. It is exclusively available through the *Kerber* publishing house.

The title of this book, *International Orange*, the color of the Golden Gate Bridge, is at the same time a reference to San Francisco, the rainbow flag of the gay movement, and an international signifier of freedom.

www.**daniel-schumann**.com